moda All-Stars

Merry MAKERS

PATCHWORK QUILTS AND PROJECTS TO CELEBRATE THE SEASON

Compiled by LISSA ALEXANDER

Martingale®
Create with Confidence

Moda All-Stars
Merry Makers: Patchwork Quilts and Projects to
Celebrate the Season
© 2018 by Martingale & Company®

Martingale®
19021 120th Ave. NE, Ste. 102
Bothell, WA 98011-9511 USA
ShopMartingale.com

Printed in China
23 22 21 20 19 18   8 7 6 5 4 3 2 1

Library of Congress Cataloging-in-Publication Data
is available upon request.

ISBN: 978-1-60468-949-5

MISSION STATEMENT

We empower makers who use fabric and yarn
to make life more enjoyable.

CREDITS

PUBLISHER AND
CHIEF VISIONARY OFFICER
Jennifer Erbe Keltner

CONTENT DIRECTOR
Karen Costello Soltys

DESIGN MANAGER
Adrienne Smitke

MANAGING EDITOR
Tina Cook

PRODUCTION MANAGER
Regina Girard

ACQUISITIONS EDITOR
Amelia Johanson

PHOTOGRAPHERS
Brent Kane
Adam Albright

TECHNICAL EDITOR
Nancy Mahoney

ILLUSTRATOR
Sandy Loi

COPY EDITOR
Durby Peterson

SPECIAL THANKS

*Thanks to the following homeowners for
allowing us to photograph in their homes:*

Ashley Carbonatto of Issaquah, Washington

*Lori Clark's The FarmHouse Cottage in
Snohomish, Washington*

Contents

Secrets from Santa

LISSA ALEXANDER

To add to the fun, each of our All-Stars shares a few holiday secrets about how they celebrate the season. My answers are below.

✳ **What is your favorite holiday treat?** The old-school Chex party mix with Poppycock Original Glazed Popcorn added.

✳ **Do you send Christmas cards, holiday emails, texts, or tweets?** Do holiday Snapchats or emojis count?

✳ **When do you open holiday gifts?** One gift on Christmas Eve, which is usually new pj's for everyone. Stockings the morning of and then gifts on Christmas Day.

✳ **Home or on the road? Where are your holidays most often spent?** The majority of my family is local, so our holiday is always at home. One son in Hawaii, so we'd all love to go there one year for Christmas.

✳ **How many trees do you decorate?** One traditional Christmas tree with all the ornaments since 1980, including many things that filled my junk drawer— golf bag tags from my husband's trips, my kids' old school IDs, tape measures, and other trinkets that are fun to see again and again each year.

✳ **What's your favorite holiday tradition?** Christmas Eve at my oldest son's home. He and his neighbors do a progressive Christmas caroling event. Once they come to your house, you can join in to visit other homes. By the end of the evening it turns into a wonderful block party.

✳ **When do you start decorating? Undecorating?** Thanksgiving night I am ready to start decorating. I keep a Pinterest board for Christmas ideas since I think about it all year long. I try and wait until New Year's Day to put things away. My mom always said it was bad luck to take Christmas down early.

✳ **What was your favorite childhood toy?** One of my brothers is two years younger, and we played together constantly. One year, Santa brought us both tea sets and baby dolls. The next year we both got train sets. So, either we fought constantly or loved the same things.

Giving Back

Is there any time of year more fun for quilters than the holiday season? There's merrymaking going on in our sewing rooms as we make gifts for those we love, merrymaking in the kitchen as we whip up family favorites, and merrymaking in our homes and offices as we gather with family and friends. And all those happy holiday feelings led us to gather our Moda all-star designers to create a collection of treats to sew, quilt, and gift to yourself and others during this special season. Most of these projects can be made in a weekend, some in an evening. And those that take a bit longer, well, those are true works of heart for those you hold dear.

In keeping with our tradition of merrily making for others, royalties for this book will be donated to Marine Toys for Tots Foundation (ToysforTots.org), which enables Toys for Tots coordinators to conduct effective local campaigns, with the goal of delivering a shiny new toy and a message of hope to needy youngsters at Christmas. And THANK YOU. Your purchase of this book will help make Christmas more merry for others.

~Lissa Alexander

Merry Gingham Lap Quilt

BY COREY YODER
quilted by Kaylene Parry

Did you know that gingham was originally striped, not checked? Here in this pretty holiday lap quilt, you can pay tribute to a classic fabric, with stripes of gingham that are easy to strip piece. How festive and fun!

FINISHED QUILT: 58¼" × 68¾"

Materials

Yardage is based on 42"-wide fabric.

¼ yard *each* of 3 different dark red prints (red background) for gingham columns

¼ yard *each* of 2 different dark green prints (green background) for gingham columns

⅜ yard *each* of 3 different medium red prints (white background with red motif) for gingham columns

⅜ yard *each* of 2 different medium green prints (white background with green motif) for gingham columns

2⅛ yards of white tone-on-tone print for background

½ yard of red stripe for binding

3⅝ yards of fabric for backing

65" × 75" piece of batting

Cutting

All measurements include ¼"-wide seam allowances.

From *each* of the dark red and dark green prints, cut:
3 strips, 2¼" × 42" (15 total)

From *each* of the medium red and medium green prints, cut:
5 strips, 2¼" × 42" (25 total)

From the white tone-on-tone print, cut:
17 strips, 2¼" × 42"
7 strips, 4" × 42"

From the red stripe, cut:
7 strips, 2¼" × 42"

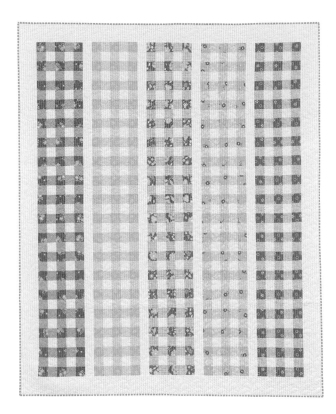

Measure Twice, Cut Once

You'll need at least 40½" of usable width to cut the required number of segments in step 1, so take care when cutting the segments. Otherwise, you may need to cut another set of strips and make a second strip set, which means you would need approximately ¼ yard more of each print.

2 Using the same medium red print used in step 1, join three medium red strips and two white 2¼" strips along their long edges, alternating the strips as shown to make a strip set that's 9¼" × 42". Crosscut the strip set into 17 segments, 2¼" × 9¼".

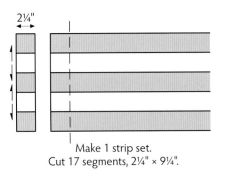

Make 1 strip set.
Cut 17 segments, 2¼" × 9¼".

Making the Columns

Press the seam allowances in the directions indicated by the arrows.

1 Choose three matching dark red strips and two matching medium red strips. Sew the strips together along their long edges, alternating the strips as shown to make a strip set that's 9¼" × 42". Crosscut the strip set into 18 segments, 2¼" × 9¼".

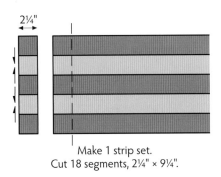

Make 1 strip set.
Cut 18 segments, 2¼" × 9¼".

3 Join the segments from steps 1 and 2, alternating them as shown, to make a red gingham column that measures 9¼" × 61¾", including seam allowances.

4 Repeat steps 1–3 to make a total of three red columns and two green columns.

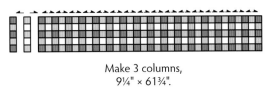

Make 3 columns,
9¼" × 61¾".

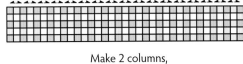

Make 2 columns,
9¼" × 61¾".

Assembling the Quilt Top

1 Join seven white 2¼"-wide strips end to end. From the pieced strip, cut four 61¾"-long strips. Beginning with a red column and alternating the colors, join the columns and sashing strips to make the quilt-top center, which should measure 51¼" × 61¾", including seam allowances.

Quilt assembly

2 Join the white 4"-wide strips end to end. From the pieced strip, cut two 61¾"-long strips and two 58¼"-long strips.

3 Sew the 61¾"-long strips to the sides of the quilt top. Sew the 58¼"-long strips to the top and bottom to complete the quilt top, which should measure 58¼" × 68¾".

Finishing

For more detailed information about any finishing steps, visit ShopMartingale.com/HowtoQuilt.

1 Layer the quilt top, batting, and backing, and quilt by hand or machine. Merry Gingham Lap Quilt is machine quilted with an allover pattern of loops and feathers.

2 Use the red stripe 2¼"-wide strips to make the binding, and then attach it to the quilt.

Secrets from Santa
COREY YODER

We're mad about plaid at the holiday season, and Corey Yoder (CorianderQuilts.com) has given us a fresh take on patchwork plaid in red and green rows. That's a wrap!

✳ **What is your favorite holiday treat?** I know you're expecting a food answer, but my favorite treat is having my husband and daughters home from work and school during the week between Christmas and New Year's Day. That's a pretty "cheesy" answer, so maybe it counts?

✳ **Do you send Christmas cards, holiday emails, texts, or tweets?** None of these. Does that make me Grinchy? To be fair, I see a lot of my friends and family during the Christmas season and wish them Merry Christmas in person.

✳ **When do you open holiday gifts?** We open gifts throughout the holiday season.

✳ **Home or on the road? Where are your holidays most often spent?** Christmas Day is spent at home.

✳ **How many trees do you decorate?** Just one!

✳ **What's your favorite holiday tradition?** Seafood extravaganza for Christmas lunch.

✳ **When do you start decorating? Undecorating?** We cut our tree down the Friday after Thanksgiving and decorate it sometime that weekend. We undecorate around New Year's Day.

✳ **What was your favorite childhood toy?** I don't own any of my childhood toys but I do remember a Malibu Barbie I had to save my money to buy. It cost me $7 and I remember saving and counting my pennies until I could purchase it.

Twinkle, Twinkle Wall Quilt

BY BARBARA GROVES AND MARY JACOBSON
quilted by Sharon Elsberry

Bright starbursts pop against a snowy white background on this Layer Cake-friendly lap quilt from Me and My Sister Designs. To add to the festive nature of the design, the quilting includes swirling motifs that are reminiscent of winter winds and Mother Nature nipping at your toes.

FINISHED QUILT: 40½" × 40½"
FINISHED BLOCK: 20" × 20"

Materials

Yardage is based on 42"-wide fabric.

8 squares, 10" × 10", of assorted red prints for blocks
8 squares, 10" × 10", of assorted green prints for blocks
2⅛ yards of white solid for blocks
⅜ yard of red dot for binding
2⅝ yards of fabric for backing
47" × 47" piece of batting
Spray starch (optional)

Cutting

All measurements include ¼"-wide seam allowances. Refer to the "Cutting for Squares" diagram on page 12 to cut all the pieces needed from the 10" squares.

From *each* red and green square, cut:
2 rectangles, 2½" × 6" (32 total)
2 rectangles, 1¼" × 7" (32 total)
2 rectangles, 1¼" × 8½" (32 total)

From the white solid, cut:
4 strips, 8⅜" × 42"; crosscut into 16 squares,
    8⅜" × 8⅜". Cut the squares in half diagonally
    to yield 32 triangles.
4 strips, 7" × 42"; crosscut into:
    32 rectangles, 3¾" × 7"
    32 rectangles, 1" × 7"
1 strip, 5½" × 42"; crosscut into 32 rectangles,
    1" × 5½"

Continued on page 12

Continued from page 11

From the red dot, cut:

5 strips, 2¼" × 42"

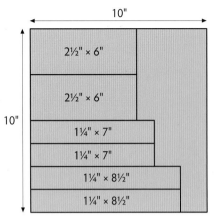

Cutting for squares

Starching Bias

Since many of the pieces in the Starburst block have bias edges, Barbara and Mary strongly recommend using a good spray starch *before* starting any cutting!

Making the Starburst Units

Instructions are for making one unit. Repeat to make 16 red and 16 green units (32 total). Sew with right sides together. Press the seam allowances in the directions indicated by the arrows.

1 From the same print, pair one red 1¼" × 7" rectangle with one red 1¼" × 8½" rectangle and pin them together. Repeat to make a total of 16 red pairs and 16 green pairs. Set the pairs aside.

2 Lay a red 2½" × 6" rectangle on your cutting mat, right side up. Using a rotary cutter and a ruler with a 45° line, align the 45° line with the lower cut edge of the rectangle. Align the edge of the ruler with the corner of the rectangle as shown. Cut along the edge of the ruler to create an angled

end. Rotate the rectangle 180°. Position the ruler as before and cut the rectangle again to make a diamond shape.

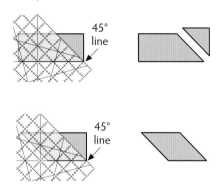

3 Sew a white 1" × 5½" rectangle to the top of the diamond from step 2 as shown. Press and trim the ends of the white rectangle even with the sides of the diamond.

4 Sew a white 1" × 7" rectangle to an adjacent side of the unit from step 3 as shown. Press and trim the ends of the white rectangle.

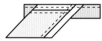 

5 Use a pair of red rectangles from step 1 that are a different print than the diamond. Sew the 1¼" × 7" rectangle to one side of the unit from step 4 as shown. Press and trim the ends of the rectangle.

6 Sew the 1¼" × 8½" rectangle to an adjacent side of the unit from step 5 as shown. Press and trim as before to complete the starburst unit. Make 16 red units.

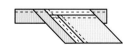 

Make 16 units.

7 Repeat steps 2–6 to make 16 green units.

Make 16 units.

Making the Blocks

1 Position the 45° line of the ruler along the lower cut edge of a white 3¾" × 7" rectangle. Align the edge of the ruler with the corner of the rectangle as shown. Cut along the edge of the ruler to create an angled end. Cut 16 A and 16 B pieces.

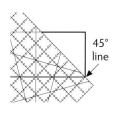

45° line

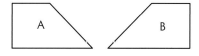

Make 16 of each unit.

2 Using eight starburst units from one color, lay out the units in a star pattern. Add four A and four B pieces as shown.

3 Sew the A and B pieces to the starburst units. The ends of the pieces should be offset as shown for sewing so that the pieces will align when pressed open. Make four of each orientation.

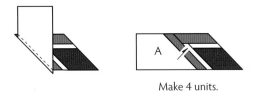

Make 4 units.

Make 4 units.

4 Sew a white triangle to each unit from step 3 as shown. Make four of each.

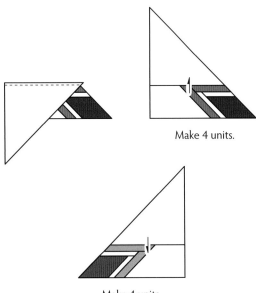

Make 4 units.

Make 4 units.

5 Join A and B units from step 4 to make four quadrants that measure 11¼" square, including seam allowances.

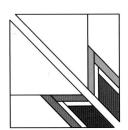 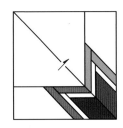

Make 4 quadrants,
11¼" × 11¼".

6 Lay out four quadrants in two rows, rotating them to form a star. Sew the quadrants together into rows. Join the rows to make a Starburst block. Make two red and two green blocks (four total). Trim and square up the blocks to measure 20½" square, including seam allowances.

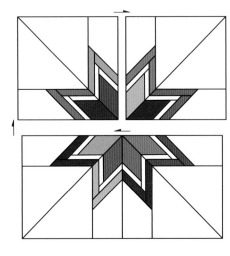

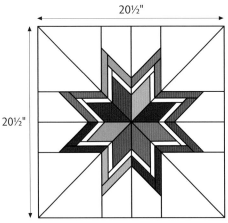

20½"

20½"

Make 2 red blocks.

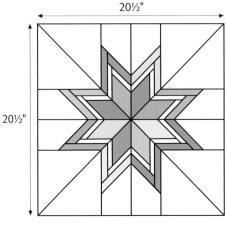

20½"

20½"

Make 2 green blocks.

Assembling the Quilt Top

1 Lay out the blocks in two rows of two blocks each. Join the blocks into rows.

2 Join the rows to complete the quilt top, which should measure 40½" square.

Quilt assembly

Finishing

For more detailed information about any finishing steps, visit ShopMartingale.com/HowtoQuilt.

1 Layer the quilt top, batting, and backing, and quilt by hand or machine. Twinkle, Twinkle Wall Quilt is machine quilted around each star with loopy lines and a heart formation of curlicues. Every other diamond piece on the inner star is quilted with either a single curlicue line or a curved line following the inside of the diamond shape.

2 Use the red dot 2¼"-wide strips to make the binding, and then attach it to the quilt.

Secrets from Santa

BARBARA GROVES AND MARY JACOBSON

They're quite a pair, just like Dasher and Dancer or Prancer and Vixen! Barbara Groves and Mary Jacobson (MeandMySisterDesigns.com) are the Me and My Sister design duo, and we can't imagine one without the other.

✳ **What is your favorite holiday treat?** An old family tradition called "gobs." Our mother has made them forever and they're gobbled up within minutes. But, that's not how they got their name. Mother says it's named after sailors called "gobs," but we've never researched it. Typically they're called whoopee pies, but we still call them gobs!

✳ **Do you send Christmas cards, holiday emails, texts, or tweets?** The tradition of mailing Christmas cards (for us) is mostly extinct. Texting is our greeting of choice.

✳ **When do you open holiday gifts?** We open one present on Christmas Eve, and the rest wait for Christmas morning.

✳ **Home or on the road? Where are your holidays most often spent?** Home!

✳ **How many trees do you decorate?** One! Who has time during the holidays to do more?

✳ **What's your favorite holiday tradition?** Both our parents have Polish traditions, and we make stuffed cabbage every Christmas Eve. It's super stinky and smells up the house, but we love eating it with lots of salt and pepper.

✳ **When do you start decorating? Undecorating?** We usually start decorating and shopping after Thanksgiving and undecorate over the New Year's holiday.

✳ **What was your favorite childhood toy?** Shrinking Violet! You'll have to Google that one. And yes, Barb does still have her.

Cheers! Bottle Bag

BY KATHY SCHMITZ

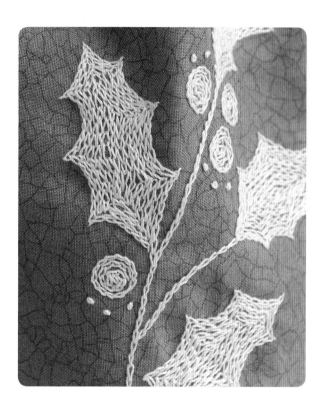

It's all in the presentation. Your holiday hostess gift will taste that much smoother when it's offered in a handmade gift bag. Pick your festive fabrics, embellish with a pretty chain-stitched holly berries motif, and whip it together in a jiffy.

FINISHED BAG: 6½" × 14½"

Materials

Yardage is based on 42"-wide fabric.

⅓ yard of green print for bag

¼ yard of coordinating plaid for bag lining and casing

12-weight ecru thread for embroidery

1¼ yards of white ½"-wide twill tape or ribbon for drawstring

Cutting

All measurements include ¼"-wide seam allowances.

From the green print, cut:
1 rectangle, 9" × 18"
1 rectangle, 7" × 15"

From the coordinating plaid, cut:
2 rectangles, 7" × 15"
2 rectangles, 2" × 6"

From the white ribbon, cut:
2 pieces, 22" long

Embroidering the Design

1 Trace the embroidery design on page 21 onto the green 9" × 18" rectangle, centering the design from side to side and placing the tip of the stem 3" from the bottom of the rectangle.

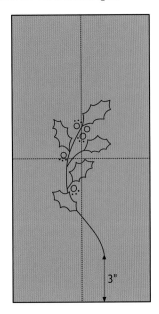

2 Using a single strand of the ecru thread, chain stitch all the lines. Fill the leaves and berries with chain stitching. Stitch French knots for the dots.

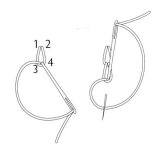

Chain stitch

French knot

3 Once the embroidery is complete, press the embroidered rectangle, embroidery side down, on a towel or other padded surface to avoid flattening the handwork.

4 Keeping the design centered, trim the embroidered rectangle to measure 7" wide. Trim the bottom edge 1" beyond the end of the stem. Trim the top so that the total length is 15". The bag front should now measure 7" × 15", including seam allowances.

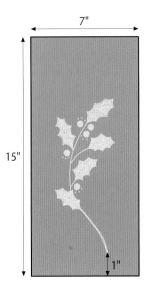

Making the Bag

Press the seam allowances in the directions indicated by the arrows.

1 Press under ½" along the short ends of a plaid 2" × 6" rectangle. Press under ¼" along the long sides to make a casing strip. Make two casing strips.

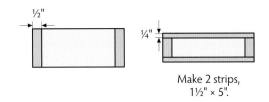

Make 2 strips,
1½" × 5".

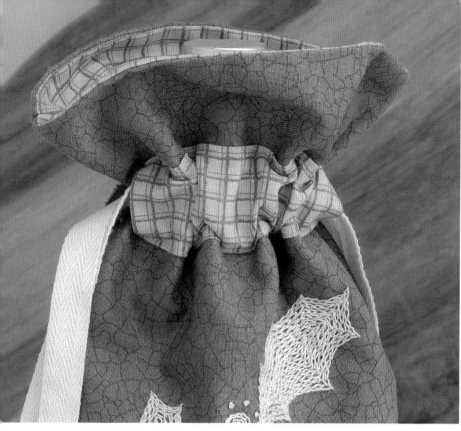

2 Pin a casing strip to the bag front, 2" from the top edge and centered from side to side. Edgestitch along the long edges of the casing. In the same way, sew the second casing strip to the green 7" × 15" rectangle to make the bag back.

3 With right sides together and using a ¼" seam allowance, sew a plaid 7" × 15" rectangle to the bag front along the top edges. Press. In the same way, sew the remaining plaid 7" × 15" rectangle to the bag back. Press.

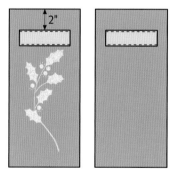

Make 1 of each unit.

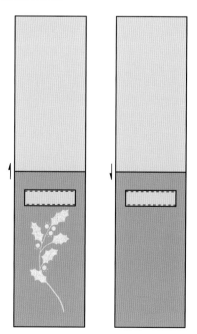

Secrets from Santa

KATHY SCHMITZ

Keeping us in stitches is what Kathy Schmitz (KathySchmitz.com) does best. Whether she's cracking corny jokes or embroidering beautiful gifts, we laugh, we sew, and so it goes!

✳ **What is your favorite holiday treat?** My grandma made THE BEST peanut butter fudge. My grandparents had a farm, and Grandma would make the fudge with fresh cream from their cows.

✳ **Do you send Christmas cards, holiday emails, texts, or tweets?** Back in the old days I always sent Christmas cards. When I stopped sending them, about eight years ago, my husband took over. Hmm . . . I wonder if that would work on laundry?

✳ **When do you open holiday gifts?** We spread out the holiday! We open stockings on the 23rd. Some presents we open on Christmas Eve with my family and some presents we open on Christmas Day with my husband's family.

✳ **Home or on the road? Where are your holidays most often spent?** Most of our relatives live an hour away, so we travel to them for both Christmas Eve and Christmas Day.

✳ **What's your favorite holiday tradition?** Opening Christmas stockings. I hand knit our stockings over 20 years ago! They're very stretchy and they hold an abundance of goodies. We take turns pulling out one item at a time. The gifts can be pretty silly, so there are always lots of laughs.

✳ **When do you start decorating? Undecorating?** We usually start the first week of December, but as soon as the calendar turns to the 26th I'm ready to put everything away.

✳ **What was your favorite childhood toy?** I really loved the Playskool camper! I played with that thing for hours. I still have it!

4 Layer the bag front and back, right sides together, aligning the plaid rectangles and nesting the seam allowances. Sew around the perimeter using a ¼" seam allowance and leaving a 4" opening along one side of the plaid rectangles.

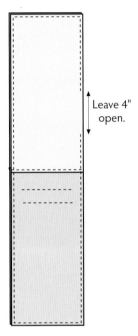

Leave 4" open.

5 Turn the bag right side out through the opening. Whipstitch the opening closed. Insert the plaid lining into the green bag; press along the top seam.

6 Using a safety pin, thread the ribbon through one of the casings, around to the other side, and then through the second casing. Repeat with the other ribbon from the opposite direction. Tie the ends of each ribbon together to form two loops.

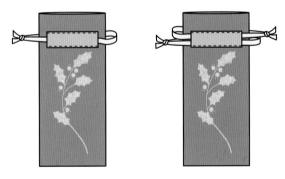

7 Insert your bottle and pull the ribbon ends to tighten the bag around the neck of the bottle for a perfect hostess gift!

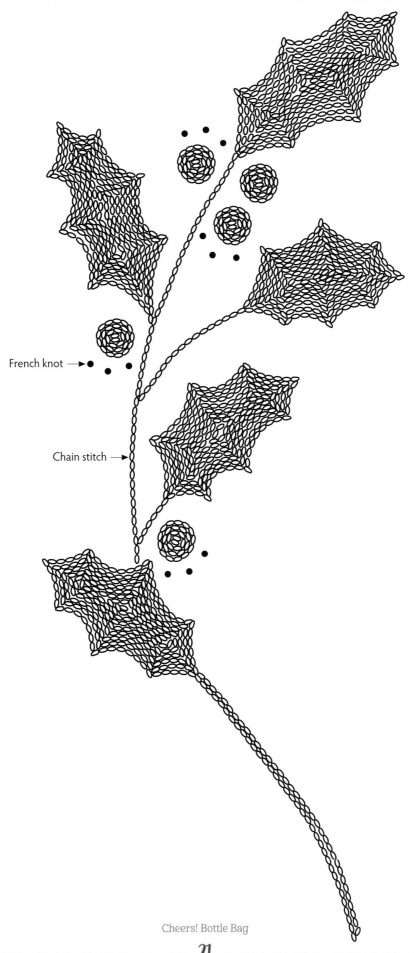

French knot →

Chain stitch →

Mini Stocking

BY JOANNA FIGUEROA

The holidays are a perfect time to sit down and work on a fun little project that gives you immediate results and versatile decorating options. The small accents on these minis make them that much more personal! Make one in a jiffy or make a dozen to decorate stairwells, trees, and doorknobs, or simply use them as sweet gifts.

FINISHED STOCKING: 6½" × 8¾"

Materials

Yardage is based on 42"-wide fabric. A fat eighth measures 9" × 21". Yields one stocking. Materials listed are for making the red check stocking.

1 fat eighth of red check for stocking
1 fat eighth of cream print for cuff
2" × 12" strip of green print for hanging loop
1 fat eighth of coordinating print for lining
¼ yard of fusible fleece
Assorted scraps of light green and tomato
    red wool for appliqués
Freezer paper

Batting Preference

Joanna loves using medium-weight fusible fleece because of its stability and fusibility. In this project, she opted for Pellon 987F Fusible Fleece. In a pinch, you can use sturdy cotton batting, such as Warm and Natural by the Warm Company.

Cutting

All measurements include ¼"-wide seam allowances. Before you begin cutting, trace the stocking pattern on page 28 onto freezer paper and cut it out. Use the template to cut the stockings from the fabrics indicated below. To cut the reverse stockings, see "Cutting the Stockings," above right. Yields one stocking.

From the red check, cut:
1 stocking
1 reversed stocking

From the cream print, cut:
1 rectangle, 7½" × 10¾"

From the green print, cut:
1 strip, 1⅜" × 12"

From the coordinating print, cut:
1 stocking
1 reversed stocking

From the fusible fleece, cut:
1 stocking
1 reversed stocking
1 rectangle, 3½" × 10¼"

Cutting the Stockings

To make a stocking, you need to cut both a front and a back (reverse) stocking piece. The simplest way to do that is to layer two pieces of fabric right sides together, place the template shape on top of the fabric pair, trace the template, and cut out both pieces at the same time. This way you'll get front and back shapes that fit together perfectly. Repeat this method for cutting the lining and fleece pieces for the stocking too.

Making the Mini Stocking

Use a ¼" seam allowance throughout. Instructions are for making one stocking.

1 Fuse the fleece stocking to the red check stocking, following the manufacturer's instructions. Fuse the reverse fleece stocking to the reverse red check stocking. Pin the prepared stocking pieces right sides together. Sew around the stocking, leaving the top edge open. Backstitch at the beginning and end of the stitched line. Clip the curves to the stitching line. Turn the stocking right side out and press.

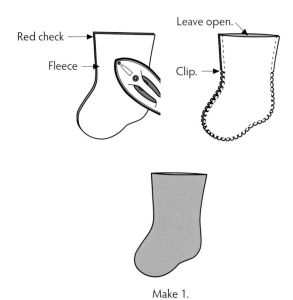

Make 1.

2 Fuse the fleece rectangle to the wrong side of the lower half of the cream rectangle. Fold the prepared cream strip in half widthwise, right sides together and short ends aligned. Sew along the short ends to make a fabric circle.

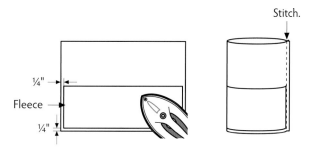

Stitch.

¼"

Fleece

¼"

3 Press the seam allowances open and then fold the fabric circle in half with the raw edges aligned to form a doubled cuff with the fusible fleece between the fabric layers; press. Machine baste around the raw edges and edgestitch along the fold.

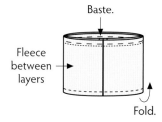

Baste.

Fleece between layers

Fold.

4 To make the hanging loop, fold the green 1⅜" × 12" strip in half lengthwise, wrong sides together, and press the fold. Unfold and turn the raw edges of the strip to the center crease; press. Refold on the center crease and press the strip. Edgestitch along the long open edge of the strip. Trim the strip to 10" long. Pin the ends together into a loop and stitch across the ends.

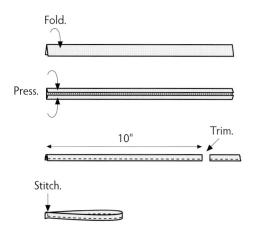

Fold.

Press.

10"

Trim.

Stitch.

Secrets from Santa

JOANNA FIGUEROA

The stockings were hung by the chimney with care, in hopes that the Fig Tree fabric fairies soon would be there . . . at least, that's what we're hoping happens when you make the adorable set of holiday stockings by designer Joanna Figueroa (FigTreeQuilts.com). Please, oh please, Santa!

✳ **What is your favorite holiday treat?** Chocolate and orange is a combination I love all year-round. At Christmas, I usually request it as a stocking stuffer. My kids get me a large orange chocolate ball that breaks into wedges when hit on the table.

✳ **When do you open holiday gifts?** We celebrate on Christmas Eve, as is Polish tradition. The big dinner, gift opening, Santa coming, caroling . . . all of it! The 25th is just a great "day after"!

✳ **Home or on the road? Where are your holidays most often spent?** We try to spend it at home as often as possible and gather everyone to us.

✳ **How many trees do you decorate?** One large noble fir in the living room. Every year in the same place. No variation on that one!

✳ **What's your favorite holiday tradition?** We follow the Polish tradition of Christmas dinner on the 24th called Vigilia. It centers around fish dishes and many salads and side dishes. The meal starts with borscht and goes for several courses while the kids wait patiently to open their presents. Dinner starts when the kids have spotted the first bright star outside and begins with the sharing of the "oplatek," a wafer blessed by the priest. It's these traditions that make Christmas so special.

✳ **When do you start decorating? Undecorating?** I decorate the day after Thanksgiving. We "deChristmas" the house on the first weekend after New Year's. My favorite decoration is a tiny Nativity set I found at a flea market about 10 years ago. It wouldn't be Christmas without it!

5 Pin the lining pieces right sides together and sew around the edges, leaving the top edge open. Clip the curves to the stitched line, but *do not* turn the lining right side out.

6 Insert the lining into the stocking, *wrong* sides together. Pin the loop to the right side of the lining, along the back seam and facing down into the stocking.

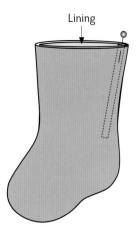

Lining

7 Place the cuff inside the lining, aligning the raw edges of the cuff with the raw edges of the lining and stocking. Align the side seamline with the back seam of the lining. Pin the cuff to the stocking and lining, easing as needed. The hanging loop should be between the lining and the cuff. Sew around the top edge, stitching through all layers—stocking, lining, and cuff. Be sure to start and stop with a backstitch. Finish the seam allowance with a zigzag stitch if desired.

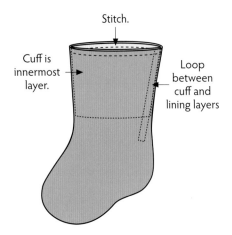

Stitch.

Cuff is innermost layer.

Loop between cuff and lining layers

8 Pull the cuff up and fold it over the top of the stocking. Pull the hanging loop up. Press the top of the stocking.

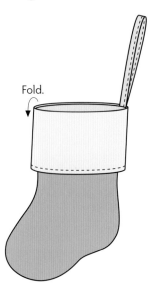

Fold.

9 Choose an appliqué design. Using the patterns on page 27 and referring to the photo on page 22 as a placement and color guide, cut the chosen pieces from the assorted wool scraps. Position and glue each piece to the cuff, let dry, and then hand appliqué using matching thread colors and a blanket stitch or whipstitch.

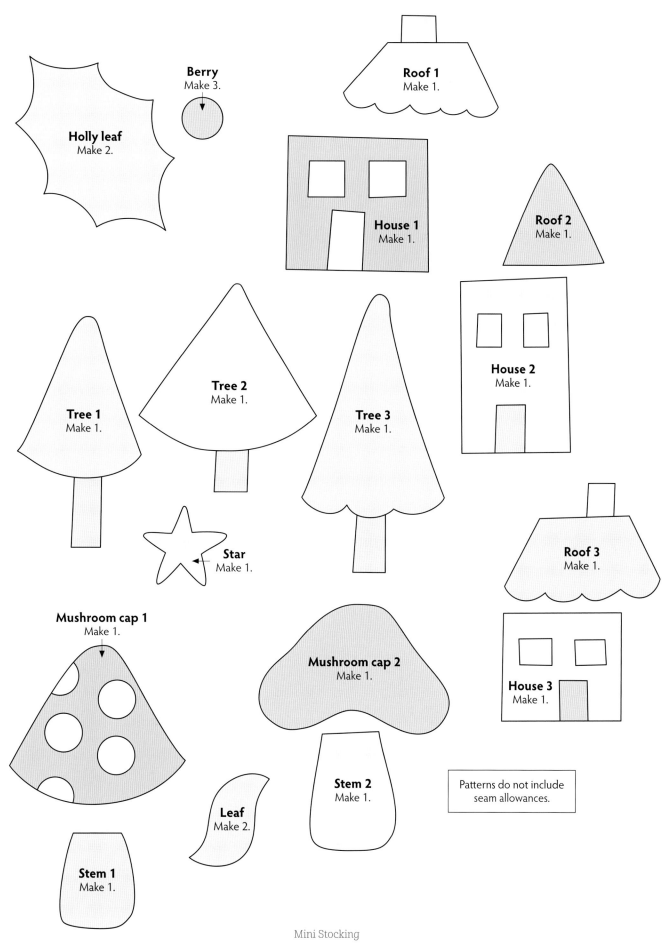

Berry
Make 3.

Holly leaf
Make 2.

Roof 1
Make 1.

House 1
Make 1.

Roof 2
Make 1.

House 2
Make 1.

Tree 1
Make 1.

Tree 2
Make 1.

Tree 3
Make 1.

Star
Make 1.

Roof 3
Make 1.

House 3
Make 1.

Mushroom cap 1
Make 1.

Mushroom cap 2
Make 1.

Stem 2
Make 1.

Leaf
Make 2.

Stem 1
Make 1.

Patterns do not include
seam allowances.

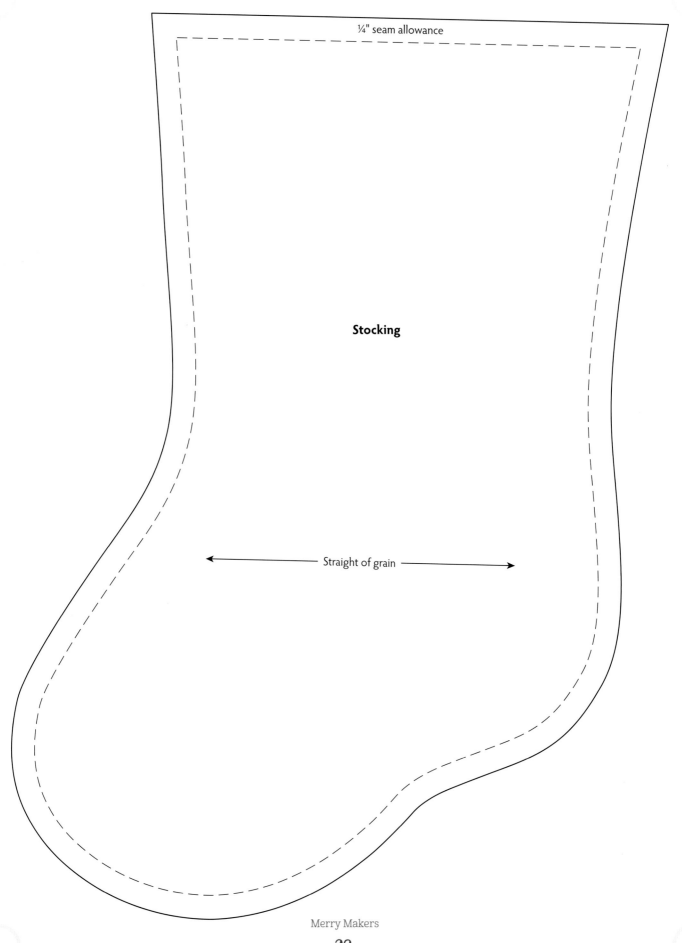

¼" seam allowance

Stocking

← Straight of grain →

Gift Wrap Lap Quilt

BY SHERRI McCONNELL
machine quilted by Marion Bott

Packages covered in bright red and green wrapping awaken our childlike wonder. So what better way to lend a little coziness and warmth this holiday season than with a quilt that's as bright and bold as a roll of Christmas gift wrap!

FINISHED QUILT: 59½" × 69½"
FINISHED BLOCKS: 5" × 5"

Materials

Yardage is based on 42"-wide fabric.

⅝ yard *each* of 6 assorted cream prints for background
½ yard *each* of 5 assorted red prints for blocks
½ yard *each* of 5 assorted green prints for blocks
½ yard of cream solid for inner border
⅞ yard of green-with-red print for outer border
½ yard of red dot for binding
3¾ yards of fabric for backing
66" × 76" piece of batting

Cutting

All measurements include ¼"-wide seam allowances.

From *each* cream print, cut:
1 strip, 6½" × 42"; crosscut into 5 squares,
    6½" × 6½" (30 total)
2 strips, 5½" × 42"; crosscut into 10 squares,
    5½" × 5½" (60 total)

From *each* red print, cut:
1 strip, 6½" × 42"; crosscut into 3 squares,
    6½" × 6½" (15 total)
2 strips, 3" × 42"; crosscut into 24 squares, 3" × 3"
    (120 total)

From *each* green print, cut:
1 strip, 6½" × 42"; crosscut into 3 squares,
    6½" × 6½" (15 total)
2 strips, 3" × 42"; crosscut into 24 squares, 3" × 3"
    (120 total)

Continued on page 31

Continued from page 29

From the cream solid, cut:

6 strips, 2" × 42"

From the green-with-red print, cut:

7 strips, 3½" × 42"

From the red dot, cut:

7 strips, 2¼" × 42"

Making the Hourglass Blocks

Press the seam allowances in the directions indicated by the arrows.

1 Draw a diagonal line from corner to corner on the wrong side of each cream print 6½" square. Place a marked square right sides together with a red 6½" square. Sew ¼" from both sides of the drawn line. Cut the unit apart on the drawn line to make two half-square-triangle units. Make 30 red and 30 green units.

Make 30 of each unit.

2 Pin two matching half-square-triangle units right sides together, nesting the seams and with contrasting colors stacked. Draw a diagonal line from corner to corner on the top unit perpendicular to the seam. Sew ¼" from both sides of the line. Cut the units apart on the drawn line to yield two Hourglass blocks. Trim to measure 5½" square, including seam allowances. Make 30 red blocks.

Make 30 blocks.

3 Repeat step 2 to make 30 green blocks that measure 5½" square.

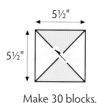

Make 30 blocks.

Making the Square-in-a-Square Blocks

1 Draw a diagonal line from corner to corner on the wrong side of four matching red 3" squares. Place a marked square on one corner of a cream print 5½" square, right sides together and raw edges aligned. Sew along the marked line. Trim the excess corner fabric, leaving a ¼" seam allowance.

2 In the same way, sew marked red squares to the remaining three corners of the cream square to make a block. Make 30 red blocks that measure 5½" square, including seam allowances.

Make 30 blocks,
5½" × 5½".

3 Repeat steps 1 and 2 using the green 3" squares and the remaining cream 5½" squares to make 30 green blocks that measure 5½" square, including seam allowances.

Make 30 blocks,
5½" × 5½".

Assembling the Quilt Top

1 Lay out six red Hourglass blocks and six red Square-in-a-Square blocks in a row, starting with an Hourglass block and alternating the blocks as shown. All of the blocks should have the same red print. Join the blocks to make a row. Make five rows that measure 5½" × 60½", including seam allowances.

2 Repeat step 1 to make five green rows, starting each row with a Square-in-a-Square block.

3 Lay out the red and green rows, alternating them as shown in the quilt assembly diagram on page 33. Join the rows to complete the quilt-top center, which should measure 50½" × 60½", including seam allowances.

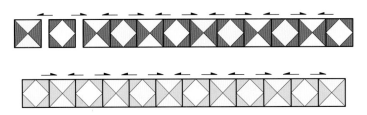

Make 5 of each row, 5½" × 60½".

4 Join the cream solid 2"-wide strips end to end. From the pieced strip, cut two 60½"-long strips and two 53½"-long strips. Sew the 60½" strips to opposite sides of the quilt top. Sew the 53½" strips to the top and bottom of the quilt top to complete the inner border. The quilt top should measure 53½" × 63½", including seam allowances.

5 Join the green-with-red strips end to end. From the pieced strip, cut two 63½"-long strips and two 59½"-long strips. Sew the 63½" strips to opposite sides of the quilt top. Sew the 59½" strips to the top and bottom of the quilt top. The quilt top should measure 59½" × 69½".

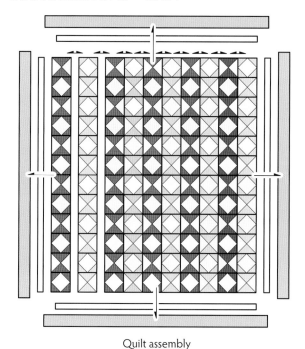

Quilt assembly

Finishing

For more detailed information about any finishing steps, visit ShopMartingale.com/HowtoQuilt.

1 Layer the quilt top, batting, and backing, and quilt by hand or machine. Gift Wrap Lap Quilt is machine quilted with an allover feather design.

2 Use the red dot 2¼"-wide strips to make the binding, and then attach it to the quilt.

Secrets from Santa

SHERRI McCONNELL

Red light, green light, dynamite, WHO? Sherri McConnell (AQuiltingLife.com), that's who! She's as sweet as candy and her quilting skills are KAPOW . . . dy-na-mite!

✳ **What is your favorite holiday treat?** See's Candy and candy canes.

✳ **Do you send Christmas cards, holiday emails, texts, or tweets?** I try to send cards but haven't done very well as of late!

✳ **When do you open holiday gifts?** Christmas morning.

✳ **Home or on the road? Where are your holidays most often spent?** Home!

✳ **How many trees do you decorate?** One or two. I have mostly handmade ornaments or ornaments that were gifts from my grandmother on our main tree.

✳ **What's your favorite holiday tradition?** Honestly, I just love seeing my children interact with one another. I'm glad they all get along so well as adults! But the Christmas dinner is probably my favorite tradition of all.

✳ **When do you start decorating? Undecorating?** I begin the day after Thanksgiving and take it all down the day after Christmas!

✳ **What was your favorite childhood toy?** I loved dollhouses, but I don't have either of the two I had anymore. (One I saved for my girls, but then we had a cat that decided to have her kittens in it.) I still have a Fisher-Price Little People Castle that all of my kids and grandchildren have played with!

On-the-Ice Table Runner

BY BRENDA RIDDLE

Icy blue Nine Patch blocks combined with natural linen, a touch of rickrack, and a nostalgic ice skate appliqué offer a welcome departure from traditional seasonal hues to make your holiday table a hit.

FINISHED TABLE RUNNER: 15½" × 67½"
FINISHED BLOCK: 3" × 3"

Materials

Yardage is based on 42"-wide fabric. Substitute cotton fabrics for felted wool if desired.

⅞ yard of light blue gingham for blocks and binding*

1⅛ yards of linen for blocks, setting squares, and appliqué background

12" × 16" rectangle of off-white felted wool for skate boots and laces

2" × 6" rectangle of dark brown or black felted wool for skate heels

6" × 6" square of gray felted wool for skate blades

1⅛ yards of fabric for backing**

20" × 72" piece of batting

1⅞ yards of off-white ½"-wide rickrack

½ yard of 17"-wide lightweight paper-backed fusible web

Thread or embroidery floss to match wool colors

*The gingham is printed diagonally, rather than woven on the straight of grain, which makes it possible to achieve a diagonal look without cutting squares or the binding on the bias.

**Brenda made extra Nine Patch blocks and used them along with leftover linen to make a pieced backing.

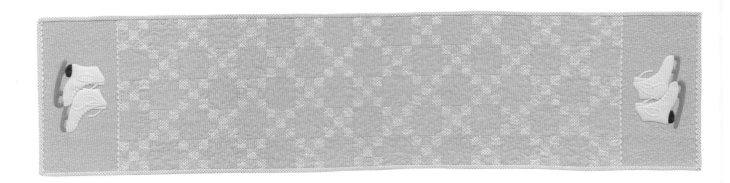

Cutting

All measurements include ¼"-wide seam allowances.

From the light blue gingham, cut:

5 strips, 2¼" × 42"

10 strips, 1½" × 42"

From the linen, cut:

1 strip, 9" × 42"; crosscut into 2 rectangles, 9" × 16"

4 strips, 3½" × 42"; crosscut into 42 squares, 3½" × 3½"

8 strips, 1½" × 42"

From the rickrack, cut:

4 pieces, 15½" long

Making the Nine Patch Blocks

Press the seam allowances in the directions indicated by the arrows.

1 Sew gingham 1½"-wide strips to both long edges of a linen 1½"-wide strip to make strip set A that measures 3½" × 42". Make four strip sets. From the strip sets, cut 86 segments, 1½" × 3½".

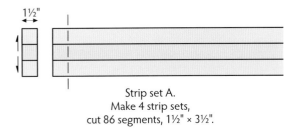

Strip set A.
Make 4 strip sets,
cut 86 segments, 1½" × 3½".

2 Sew linen 1½"-wide strips to both long edges of a gingham 1½"-wide strip to make strip set B that measures 3½" × 42". Make two strip sets. From the strip sets, cut 43 segments, 1½" × 3½".

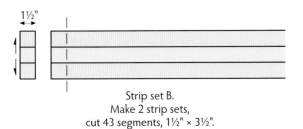

Strip set B.
Make 2 strip sets,
cut 43 segments, 1½" × 3½".

3 Join A segments to both sides of a B segment to make a Nine Patch block that measures 3½" square. Make a total of 43 blocks.

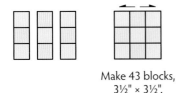

Make 43 blocks,
3½" × 3½".

Appliquéing the End Units

If you choose to appliqué the blocks using cotton fabrics, use your preferred appliqué method. The following instructions are for wool appliqué.

1 Using the patterns on page 39, trace two sets of each element (skate boots, laces, heel, blades) onto the paper side of fusible web. Note that the patterns have been reversed for fusible appliqué.

Roughly cut out the paper shapes, leaving about ¼" outside the traced lines. Following the manufacturer's instructions, press the shapes onto the wrong side of the appropriate colors of felted wool. Cut out the shapes on the traced line and sort the pieces for each set of skates.

2 Use the pattern as a placement guide to arrange one set of wool shapes on a linen 9" × 16" rectangle, centering the appliqué design. Remove the paper backing as you place the shapes onto the linen. When you're pleased with the arrangement, carefully press the wool shapes to the linen rectangle.

3 Using a hand or machine blanket stitch or whipstitch and a thread color to match the wool, stitch around the edges of the wool shapes. (For the sample, Brenda stitched around all the shapes, except the laces, using a small machine blanket stitch. For the laces, she worked a small whipstitch by hand using a single strand of embroidery floss.) Make two end units and trim them to 8½" × 15½", including seam allowances.

4 Place a length of rickrack along one long edge of an appliquéd end unit, centering it from side to side. Stitch through the center of the rickrack using off-white thread. Sew a second length of rickrack to the opposite side of the appliquéd unit. Repeat to add rickrack trim to the second end unit.

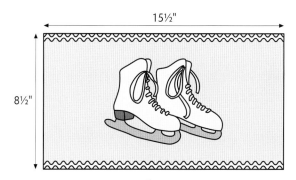

15½"

8½"

Make 2 units.

Secrets from Santa

BRENDA RIDDLE

We'd be skating on thin ice if we said any but nice things about Brenda Riddle's designs (AcornQuiltandGiftCompany.com). Her charming figures are always fabulous—whether she's skating or quilting.

✳ **What is your favorite holiday treat?** Peppermint anything!

✳ **Do you send Christmas cards, holiday emails, texts, or tweets?** Christmas cards and emails too.

✳ **When do you open holiday gifts?** Christmas morning.

✳ **Home or on the road? Where are your holidays most often spent?** Home sweet home.

✳ **How many trees do you decorate?** One or two. Usually one traditionally and then one for the kitchen, but I'm still collecting things for that tree.

✳ **What's your favorite holiday tradition?** Christmas Eve service at church.

✳ **When do you start decorating? Undecorating?** I start the weekend after Thanksgiving. Usually within a week after Christmas I start to take things down. It's so nice to start the New Year with a clean, fresh house.

✳ **What was your favorite childhood toy?** I still have a Winnie-the-Pooh from when I was little. And I still love it.

Assembling the Table Runner

1 Sew three Nine Patch blocks and two linen squares together, alternating them as shown. Make nine rows that measure 3½" × 15½", including seam allowances.

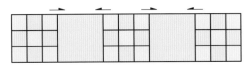

Make 9 rows,
3½" × 15½".

2 Sew three linen squares and two Nine Patch blocks together, alternating them as shown. Make eight rows that measure 3½" × 15½", including seam allowances.

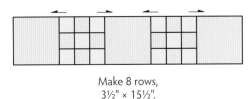

Make 8 rows,
3½" × 15½".

3 Join the rows from steps 1 and 2, alternating them as shown in the table-runner assembly diagram. The table runner should measure 15½" × 51½", including seam allowances.

4 Sew an appliquéd end unit to each end of the table runner to complete the table-runner top. The table runner should measure 15½" × 67½".

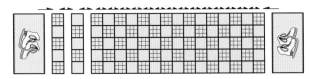

Table-runner assembly

Finishing

For more detailed information about any finishing steps, visit ShopMartingale.com/HowtoQuilt.

1 Layer the runner top, batting, and backing, and quilt by hand or machine. On-the-Ice Table Runner is machine quilted with an allover meandering pattern.

2 Use the gingham 2¼"-wide strips to make the binding, and then attach it to the runner.

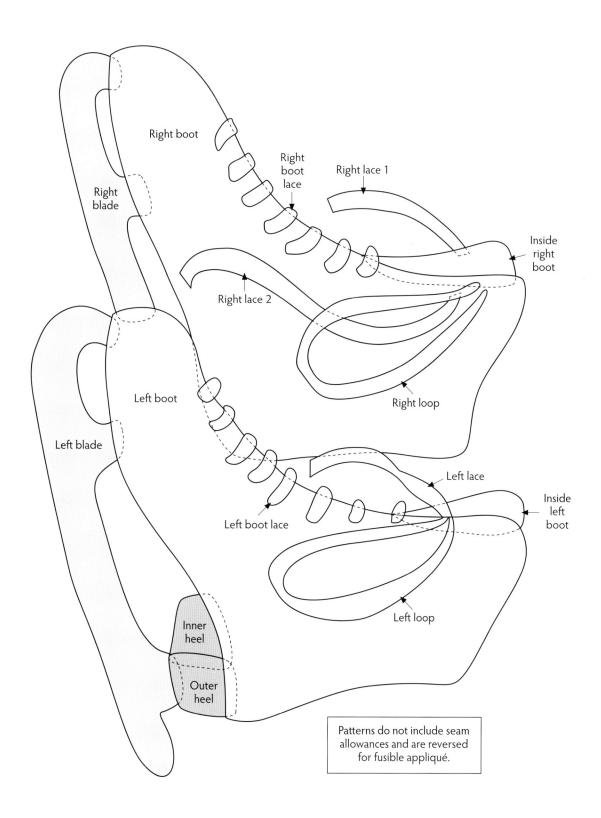

Right boot

Right
blade

Right
boot
lace

Right lace 1

Inside
right
boot

Right lace 2

Right loop

Left boot

Left lace

Inside
left
boot

Left blade

Left boot lace

Left loop

Inner
heel

Outer
heel

Patterns do not include seam
allowances and are reversed
for fusible appliqué.

Perpetual Holiday Wreath

BY JANE DAVIDSON

Make a seasonal wreath using three-dimensional fabric flowers in colors to reflect your favorite holidays. The flowers are pinned to a wreath form with decorative centers, so you can change them out to celebrate every season.

FINISHED WREATH: 13" diameter

Materials

Yardage is based on 42"-wide fabric.

35 squares, 10" × 10", of assorted light, medium, and dark prints for flower petals and flower centers

½ yard of navy fabric for covering the wreath form

12-weight cotton thread for gathering flower petals

50-weight thread for appliquéd flower centers

Heat-resistant template plastic

Spray starch

Appliqué glue

1 foam craft wreath, approximately 12" to 13" diameter

40" of navy ¼"-wide ribbon

1 box of shirt pins (300–500 count, 26 mm × 0.65 mm) *OR* sequin and bead pins (300–500 count, 16 mm × 0.65 mm)

1 packet of flower sequins (500 count, 5 mm to 10 mm)

Sequins and Pins

Search online for flower sequins, sequin pins, or beading pins to find suppliers. Sequin and beading pins have large heads, which helps secure the sequin to the wreath.

Cutting

All measurements include ¼"-wide seam allowances. Before cutting, choose 31 squares for the flower petals and 4 squares for the flower centers. Using the patterns on page 45, trace 1 large and 10 small circles onto the heat-resistant template plastic and cut them out. Use the templates to cut the large and small circles from the fabrics indicated below.

From *each* of the 31 squares for flower petals, cut:
5 large circles (155 total)

From the 4 squares for flower centers, cut a *total* of:
31 small circles

From the navy fabric, cut:
5 strips, 2½" × 42"

Circles from Squares

When using 10" squares, don't just start randomly cutting circles. First, use the large-circle pattern to trace five circles as shown in the cutting guide below. That way you're sure you can cut the number of circles needed from each square.

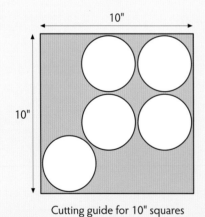

Cutting guide for 10" squares

Making Flower A

1 Select five matching large circles. Fold each circle in half, wrong sides together.

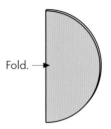

Fold. →

2 Thread a needle with a 12" length of 12-weight thread and knot one end. Starting on the back of a folded circle, sew a running stitch ¼" from the raw edge. The more stitches sewn, the more pleats you have. Be consistent in the number of running stitches for each petal so they look similar. Tightly pull the thread to gather the half circle.

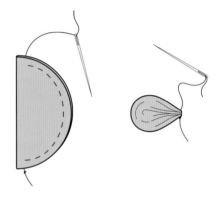

3 Using the same thread, continue sewing a running stitch along the raw edges of the other four matching folded circles, gathering each petal before adding the next one. Tightly pull both ends of the thread to form a flower. Tie multiple knots to secure the flower. Make 15 A flowers.

Flower A.
Make 15.

Making Flower B

1 Select five matching large circles. Fold each circle in half, wrong sides together. Then fold each circle in half again.

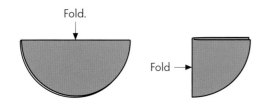

Fold.

Fold →

2 Follow steps 2 and 3 of "Making Flower A" on page 42 to make 16 B flowers.

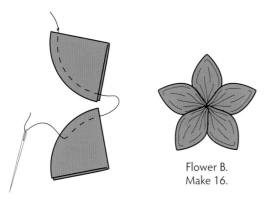

Flower B.
Make 16.

Making the Flower Centers

1 Use a needle and thread to sew a small running stitch ⅛" from the raw edge of a small circle. Do not clip the thread. Place a small-circle plastic template in the center of the fabric circle. Pull the thread tails to snugly gather the thread around the template, making sure the edges are smooth. Knot the thread. Generously spray both sides of the circle with starch. Press and let dry. Clip a few stitches to release the seam and gently remove the plastic template. Make 31 flower centers.

 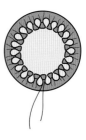

Flower center.
Make 31.

Secrets from Santa

JANE DAVIDSON

It's not fair for us, but Jane Davidson (QuiltJane.com) always gets to open her presents first . . . maybe that's because she's in Australia and Christmas comes first to her! Regardless, Santa loves the Aussie, Aussie, Aussie, oy, oy, oy so much, he asked us to share her responses exactly as submitted. You'll have to add in the Aussie accent as you read.

✳ **What is your favorite holiday treat?** Pistachio, cranberry, and white chocolate cookies.

✳ **Do you send Christmas cards, holiday emails, texts, or tweets?** I do a combination of sending emails and calling loved ones by phone.

✳ **When do you open holiday gifts?** On Christmas Day if I'm good, but straightaway if I'm naughty.

✳ **Home or on the road? Where are your holidays most often spent?** Between Sydney and Brisbane.

✳ **How many trees do you decorate?** Two— one large and one small.

✳ **What's your favorite holiday tradition?** I host a tree-trimming party. We invite everyone over for a party, unbox the decorations, and let each person choose one and place it on the tree. A friend of many years introduced me to this wonderful tradition.

✳ **When do you start decorating? Undecorating?** I start decorating on November 1st. And as far as undecorating, well I've been naughty some years and left the tree up for Christmas in July.

✳ **What was your favorite childhood toy?** LEGO. And, yes, I still have all my LEGO bricks boxed away!

2 Place a few drops of appliqué glue on the back of a flower center and position it in the center of a flower. Using a small appliqué stitch and matching 50-weight thread, appliqué the flower center in place.

Flower A.
Make 15.

Flower B.
Make 16.

Assembling the Wreath

1 Join the navy 2½" × 42" strips end to end. Press the seam allowances open.

2 Fold one end over ¼" and pin it to the back of the foam wreath. Start wrapping the strip around the wreath, overlapping the fabric with each turn. Keep wrapping until the foam wreath is covered. Finish at the back of the foam wreath. Fold the end over ¼" and insert a few pins to hold it in place.

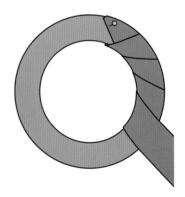

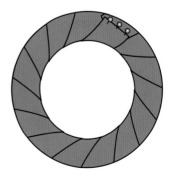

3 Tie the navy ribbon into a loop at the top of the wreath.

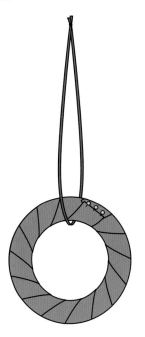

4 Referring to the photo on page 40, pin two rows of flowers around the wreath, using one pin and one sequin for each flower. Pin 14 flowers for the inner row and 17 flowers for the outer row. When happy with the layout of the flowers, pin at least six to eight more sequins to each flower to hold the flowers securely in place.

Make It Your Own

Instead of sequins, you can substitute pearl-headed pins or individual elements from decorative trimmings if you like.

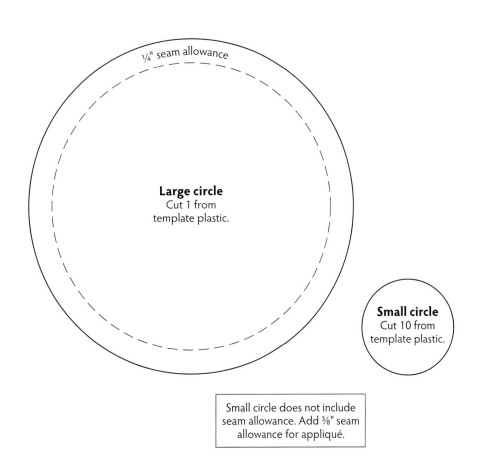

¼" seam allowance

Large circle
Cut 1 from
template plastic.

Small circle
Cut 10 from
template plastic.

Small circle does not include
seam allowance. Add ⅜" seam
allowance for appliqué.

Christmastide Coasters

BY JO MORTON

These coasters are made in festive colors for the holiday season, and they can be used for more than just beverages. Jo uses one as a perch for her pincushion and scissors when hand stitching. It's a joyous little reminder of the season, and it protects the surface of her reproduction table.

FINISHED COASTERS: 4½" × 4½"
FINISHED BLOCKS: 4" × 4"

Materials

Yardage is based on 42"-wide fabric. A fat eighth measures 9" × 21". Yields four coasters.

1 fat eighth of olive green print A for blocks and binding

2" × 10" strip of olive green print B for Broken Dishes block

1 rectangle, 5" × 13", *each* of 2 different tan prints for blocks

1 square, 4" × 4", *each* of 2 different tan prints for Sawtooth Star blocks

3" × 6" rectangle of tan plaid for Sawtooth Star blocks

1 fat eighth of red print A for blocks and binding

5" × 5" square of red print B for Broken Dishes blocks

5" × 10" rectangle of red print C for Broken Dishes blocks

1 strip, 2½" × 21", *each* of 2 different dark green prints for binding

4 squares, 6" × 6", of fabric for backing

4 squares, 6" × 6", of batting

Cutting for Sawtooth Star Coasters

Yields two coasters.

From olive green print A, cut:
4 squares, 1⅞" × 1⅞"
2 strips, 1⅛" × 21"*

From *each* of 2 tan print rectangles, cut:
1 square, 3¼" × 3¼" (2 total)

From *each* of 2 tan print squares, cut:
4 squares, 1½" × 1½" (8 total)

From the tan plaid rectangle, cut:
2 squares, 2½" × 2½"

From red print A, cut:
4 squares, 1⅞" × 1⅞"
2 strips, 1⅛" × 21"*

*Depending on the width of your strips, you may need only 1 strip from each fabric.

Cutting for Broken Dishes Coasters

Yields two coasters.

From *each* of 2 tan print rectangles, cut:
2 squares, 4½" × 4½" (4 total)

From *each* of red print A and B, cut:
1 square, 4½" × 4½" (2 total)

From red print C, cut:
2 squares, 4½" × 4½"

From *each* of olive green print A and B, cut:
1 rectangle, 1" × 4½" (2 total)
2 rectangles, 1" × 2¼" (4 total)

From *each* dark green print, cut:
2 strips, 1⅛" × 21" (4 total)*

*Depending on the width of your strips, you may need only 1 strip.

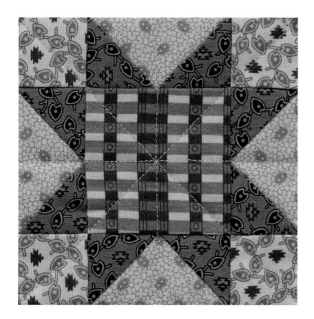

Making the Sawtooth Star Blocks

Press the seam allowances in the directions indicated by the arrows.

1 Draw a diagonal line from corner to corner on the wrong side of the olive green A 1⅞" squares. Align two squares on opposite corners of a tan 3¼" square, right sides together. The marked squares should overlap in the center. Sew a scant ¼" from both sides of the drawn line. Cut the unit apart on the drawn line to make two units.

2 Place a marked square on the corner of a large triangle from step 1, right sides together, noting the direction of the marked line. Sew a scant ¼" from both sides of the drawn line. Cut the unit apart on the drawn line. Repeat with the remaining marked square and unit from step 1 to yield four flying-geese units. The units should measure 1½" × 2½", including seam allowances.

Make 4 units,
1½" × 2½".

3 Arrange four tan 1½" squares, the flying-geese units, and a tan plaid 2½" square as shown. Sew the units together into rows. Join the rows, matching the seam intersections, to make a Sawtooth Star block that measures 4½" square.

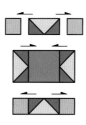

Make 1 block,
4½" × 4½".

4 Repeat steps 1–3 using the red print A squares, the remaining tan print 3¼" square and tan print 1½" squares, and the remaining tan plaid 2½" square to make the second Sawtooth Star block.

Make 1 block,
4½" × 4½".

Clipping Trick

To create a coaster with a nice, flat surface on which to set beverages, clip the seam allowances on the wrong side of each block as shown. Press the background corners toward the corner and the center section toward the center. Press the seam intersections open.

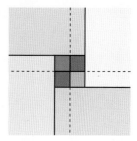

Making the Broken Dishes Blocks

Press the seam allowances in the directions indicated by the arrows.

1 Draw a diagonal line from corner to corner in both directions to form an X on the wrong side of each tan 4½" square. Place the marked square on top of a red A square, right sides together. Sew ¼" from both sides of the drawn lines. Cut the units apart horizontally and vertically. Then cut the units apart on the drawn lines to yield eight half-square triangles. Trim each unit to 1⅜" square. Repeat to make eight half-square-triangle units using a marked tan square and the red B square (use the same tan print as for the A half-square-triangle units). Make 16 half-square-triangle units using the two remaining marked tan squares and the red C squares.

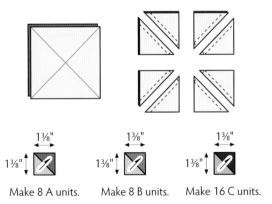

Make 8 A units.   Make 8 B units.   Make 16 C units.

2 Arrange two A and two C units in two rows as shown. Sew the units together into rows. Join the rows, nesting the center seam (see "Clipping Trick" on page 49). The broken-dishes unit should measure 2¼" square, including seam allowances. Make four units.

Make 4 units,
2¼" × 2¼".

3 Repeat step 2 using two B and two C units to make four broken-dishes units that measure 2¼" square, including seam allowances.

Make 4 units,
2¼" × 2¼".

4 Arrange two units from step 2, two units from step 3, two olive green 1" × 2¼" rectangles, and one olive green 1" × 4½" rectangle as shown. Sew a short olive green rectangle between two units to make a 2¼" × 4½" row. Make two rows. Sew a row on each side of the long olive green rectangle to make a block. Make two blocks that measure 4½" square.

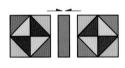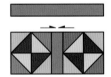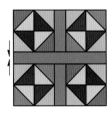

Make 2 blocks,
4½" × 4½".

Finishing

For more detailed information about any finishing steps, visit ShopMartingale.com/HowtoQuilt.

1 Layer a block, batting square, and backing square, and quilt by hand or machine. The coasters are machine quilted from corner to corner, through the center of the green sashing on the Broken Dishes coasters, and across the center of the Sawtooth Star coasters.

2 Use the red 1⅛"-wide strips to make single-fold binding, and then attach it to one of the Sawtooth Star coasters. In the same way, use the olive green 1⅛"-wide strips to bind the other Sawtooth Star coaster. Use two matching dark green strips to bind one of the Broken Dishes coasters. Use the remaining dark green strips to bind the other Broken Dishes coaster.

Reduce the Bulk

Because you want coasters to be flat to reduce accidental tip overs, try single-fold binding. It's much less bulky than traditional double-fold binding and looks beautiful on petite quilts and one-block coasters.

Secrets from Santa

JO MORTON

For a minute there, we thought Jo Morton (JoMortonQuilts.com) was coasting on her project. Then we realized, what luck! It's a set of beautiful coasters! Genius!

✳ **What is your favorite holiday treat?** Peanut brittle. A friend gifts us with a small package every Christmas.

✳ **Do you send Christmas cards, holiday emails, texts, or tweets?** No Christmas cards for some years. Sometimes I send a group holiday email to my first cousins. No texts or tweets.

✳ **When do you open holiday gifts?** We don't exchange gifts. When we first got married, it wasn't in the budget. When the budget did allow, we were used to our habits. Instead, when we vacation, if we find something we love and think it works in our home, we buy it. We don't wait for the holidays—we're making memories!

✳ **Home or on the road? Where are your holidays most often spent?** Home.

✳ **How many trees do you decorate?** One. However, the past couple of years we have just enjoyed the lit tree without ornaments. The tree has a nice glow in the family room. That seems to work, over hours of placing ornaments just right.

✳ **What's your favorite holiday tradition?** We like to go to Omaha and enjoy the sights and sounds in the Old Market or meet up with our friends from Illinois at the Plaza in Kansas City.

✳ **When do you start decorating? Undecorating?** One year with a Jo's Little Women Club deadline looming, I decorated on December 23rd. Most years I try to decorate the day after Thanksgiving.

Winterlude Lap Quilt

BY BETSY CHUTCHIAN; quilted by Sheri Mecom

Showcase a gorgeous print and perfect your technique for making half-square-triangle units by creating a warm and welcoming quilt. Need to finish in a pinch? Just substitute solid strips or a mini print for the pieced inner border. Either way, a quilt is an unbeatable gift.

FINISHED QUILT: 36¾" × 48⅛"
FINISHED BLOCK: 8" × 8"

Materials

Yardage is based on 42"-wide fabric.

½ yard *each* of 3 assorted cream prints for blocks and pieced border

¼ yard *each* of 6 assorted navy prints for blocks and pieced border

1½ yards of blue floral for setting squares and triangles, outer border, and binding

2½ yards of fabric for backing

43" × 55" piece of batting

Cutting

All measurements include ¼"-wide seam allowances.

From *each* cream print, cut:

2 strips, 2⅝" × 42"; crosscut into:
    26 squares, 2⅝" × 2⅝" (78 total; 2 will be extra)
    2 squares, 2⅛" × 2⅛" (6 total; 2 will be extra)

2 squares, 5¼" × 5¼"; cut the squares into quarters diagonally to yield 8 B triangles (24 total)

2 squares, 3⅜" × 3⅜"; cut the squares into quarters diagonally to yield 8 D triangles (24 total)

8 squares, 2½" × 2½" (24 total)

8 squares, 2" × 2" (24 total)

8 squares, 1½" × 1½" (24 total)

Continued on page 54

Continued from page 53

From *each* navy print, cut:

13 squares, 2⅝" × 2⅝" (78 total; 2 will be extra)

1 square, 2½" × 2½" (6 total)

8 squares, 2" × 2"; cut *4 of the squares* in half diagonally to yield 8 C triangles (48 triangles total and 24 squares remaining)

8 squares, 1⅞" × 1⅞"; cut the squares in half diagonally to yield 16 A triangles (96 total)

From the blue floral, cut:

2 squares, 13" × 13"; cut the squares into quarters diagonally to yield 8 side triangles (2 will be extra)

2 squares, 8½" × 8½"

2 squares, 7½" × 7½"; cut the squares in half diagonally to yield 4 corner triangles

4 strips, 4" × 42"

5 strips, 2¼" × 42"

Making the Blocks

Each block consists of one cream print and one navy print. Instructions are for making one block. Repeat to make six blocks. Press the seam allowances in the directions indicated by the arrows.

1 Draw a diagonal line from corner to corner on the wrong side of four matching cream 2" squares. Place each marked square right sides together with a navy 2" square. Sew ¼" from both sides of the drawn line. Cut the unit apart on the drawn line to make two half-square-triangle units. Press, then trim the units to measure 1½" square, including seam allowances. Make eight half-square-triangle units.

Make 8 units.

2 Sew two matching navy A triangles to each half-square-triangle unit as shown. Make eight pieced triangle units.

Make 8 units.

3 Sew two units from step 2 to the short edges of a cream B triangle as shown to make a side unit. Make four units that measure 2½" × 4½", including seam allowances.

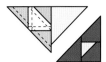

Make 4 units,
2½" × 4½".

4 Sew two navy C triangles to the short edges of a cream D triangle to make a flying-geese unit. Trim the unit to measure 1½" × 2½", including seam allowances. Make four units.

Make 4 units.

5 Arrange four cream 1½" squares, the flying-geese units, and one navy 2½" square in three rows as shown. Sew the pieces together into rows. Join the rows to make a center-star unit that measures 4½" square, including seam allowances.

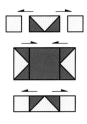

Make 1 unit,
4½" × 4½".

6 Lay out four cream 2½" squares, the side units from step 3, and the center-star unit in three rows as shown. Sew the pieces together into rows. Join the rows to make a block that measures 8½" square, including seam allowances. Repeat all steps to make a total of six blocks.

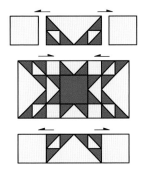 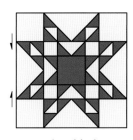

Make 6 blocks,
8½" × 8½".

Making the Pieced Borders

1 Draw a diagonal line from corner to corner on the wrong side of each cream 2⅝" square. Place a marked square right sides together with a navy 2⅝" square. Sew ¼" from both sides of the drawn line. Cut the unit apart on the drawn line to make two half-square-triangle units. Trim the units to measure 2⅛" square, including seam allowances. Make 152 half-square-triangle units.

Make 152 units.

2 Lay out two rows of 21 half-square-triangle units, making sure to orient the units as shown. Sew the units together into rows. Join the rows to make a side border. Make two borders that measure 3¾" × 34⅝", including seam allowances.

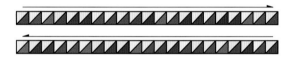

Make 2 side borders, 3¾" × 34⅝".

3 Lay out two rows of 17 half-square-triangle units and one cream 2⅛" square each, making sure to orient the units as shown. Sew the units and squares together into rows. Join the rows to make a top border. Repeat to make the bottom border. The borders should measure 3¾" × 29¾", including seam allowances.

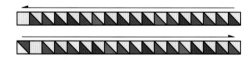

Make 2 top/bottom borders, 3¾" × 29¾".

Assembling the Quilt Top

1 Lay out the blocks, blue floral squares, side triangles, and corner triangles in diagonal rows as shown. Sew the blocks, squares, and side triangles together into rows. Join the rows, adding the corner triangles last to make the quilt-top center. The side and corner triangles were cut a bit oversized for easier cutting and piecing. Trim and square up the quilt-top center to measure 23¼" × 34⅝", making sure to leave at least ¼" beyond the points of the blocks for seam allowances.

Quilt assembly

2 Sew the pieced side borders to opposite sides of the quilt-top center. Sew the pieced top and bottom borders to the top and bottom of the quilt top. The quilt top should measure 29¾" × 41⅛", including seam allowances.

3 Measure the length of the quilt top. Cut two strips to this measurement from the blue 4"-wide strips, piecing the strips as needed. Sew the strips to opposite sides of the quilt top.

4 Measure the width of the quilt top, including the side borders. Cut two strips to this measurement from the remaining blue 4"-wide strips. Sew the strips to the top and bottom of the quilt top, which should measure 36¾" × 48⅛".

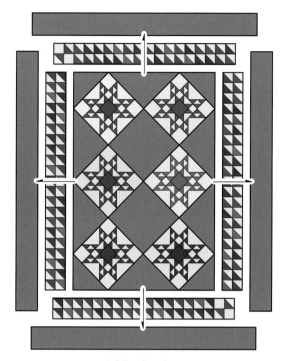

Adding borders

Finishing

For more detailed information about any finishing steps, visit ShopMartingale.com/HowtoQuilt.

1 Layer the quilt top, batting, and backing, and quilt by hand or machine. Winterlude Lap Quilt is machine quilted with curves in the inner border, a curved grid in the setting squares and triangles, and feathers in the blocks and outer border.

2 Use the blue 2¼"-wide strips to make the binding, and then attach it to the quilt.

Secrets from Santa

BETSY CHUTCHIAN

Star light, star bright, the wish we wish tonight is that our star-studded Winterlude quilt looks as spectacular as star quilter Betsy Chutchian's (BetsysBestQuiltsandMore.blogspot.com) does!

✳ **What is your favorite holiday treat?** I like sweet and salty treats. Toffee for sweet, and Texas Trash (original made-in-the-oven Chex Mix) for salty.

✳ **Do you send Christmas cards, holiday emails, texts, or tweets?** My husband sends cards every year. I email or text.

✳ **When do you open holiday gifts?** Christmas morning.

✳ **Home or on the road? Where are your holidays most often spent?** I've hosted Christmas for 38 years, and I'm very ready to pass the tradition to my daughter.

✳ **How many trees do you decorate?** Several years ago we switched from one great big tree to five 4' to 5' trees. I decorate each one differently, from a traditional green tree all decked out with Santas, red balls, beads, and white lights in the living room to a white feather tree with colorful antique glass balls in the dining room.

✳ **What's your favorite holiday tradition?** I make a lot of cookies and candy for the holidays, but the first sweet I make has to be Christmas tree cookies made with my mom's cookie press. I made them with my mom, then with my kids, and now with my grandkids.

✳ **When do you start decorating? Undecorating?** I like to start decorating as soon after Thanksgiving as possible. I undecorate before New Year's Day because my mom said it was bad luck to still have the tree up January 1.

Special Delivery Gift-Card Holder

BY KARLA EISENACH

A gift card will never seem like a last-minute effort when it's tucked inside a handmade holder. These adorable little quilted envelopes are ideal scrap projects. They not only lend a personal touch to your gift but can be tucked in a purse or bag to hold business cards long after the gift card has been spent.

FINISHED SIZE: 4¾" × 3", closed; 4¾" × 6", open

Materials

Yields one gift-card holder.

Scraps, at least 6" × 8", of 4 different coordinating prints for front and back

1 strip, 2¼" × 30", of coordinating fabric for binding

6" × 8" rectangle of batting

1 small snap for closure

1 button, ⅞" diameter or smaller, for embellishment

Cutting

All measurements include ¼"-wide seam allowances. Yields one gift-card holder.

From the 4 coordinating prints, cut a *total* of:

1 rectangle, 6" × 8"

1 rectangle, 4¾" × 6"

2 squares, 3" × 3"

1 square, 2" × 2"

Calling All Scraps

Even if you're not a scrap quilter, this quick-as-a-wink card holder will have you holding onto your favorite bits of fabric. Make a list and check it twice—hairstylists, mail carriers, teachers, house cleaners—all will appreciate your thoughtfulness.

Making the Gift-Card Holder

1 Place the print 6" × 8" rectangle wrong side up on a flat surface. Center the batting rectangle on top of the fabric rectangle. Center the print 4¾" × 6" rectangle on top of the batting, right side up. Machine quilt the layers in a crosshatch pattern, spacing the stitched lines 1" apart. Trim the excess batting and large rectangle even with the top rectangle.

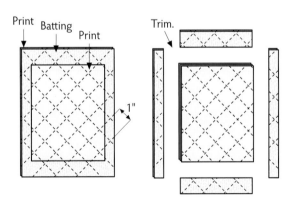

Print Batting
        Print   Trim.

1"

2 To make the inside pocket, fold each print 3" square in half diagonally, wrong sides together, to make two folded triangles.

Fold.

Make 2.

3 Place the folded triangles on the bottom corners of the quilted rectangle, matching the raw edges and overlapping the triangles in the center. Machine baste along the raw edges to hold the triangles in place.

Baste.

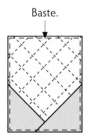

Merry Makers

4 Use the print 2¼"-wide strip to make the binding, and then attach it to the quilted rectangles. For detailed information about binding, visit ShopMartingale.com/HowtoQuilt.

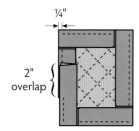

¼"

2" overlap

5 For the outside patch, turn under ¼" along each edge of the print 2" square and press. Place the patch on the outside lower-right corner of the quilted rectangle and hand stitch in place. Sew the button to the patch for embellishment.

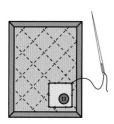

6 Sew one side of the snap to the inside top edge of the quilted rectangle just below the binding. Sew the other side of the snap to the bottom edge of the inside pocket to complete the gift-card holder.

Snap

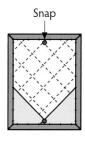

7 Fold the holder in half and snap together. Steam press the holder to crease the fold. Place a gift card in the pocket.

Secrets from Santa

KARLA EISENACH

Who wants to be on Karla Eisenach's (TheSweetwaterCo.com) gift-card list? We do! We do! A perpetual name on Santa's "Nice List," Karla is always thinking of others. Sweet!

✳ **What is your favorite holiday treat?** Frosted sugar cookies.

✳ **Do you send Christmas cards, holiday emails, texts, or tweets?** When I send, it's cards. But, sadly, I haven't sent any for a few years.

✳ **When do you open holiday gifts?** Christmas Day, starting with the youngest and working our way to the oldest.

✳ **Home or on the road? Where are your holidays most often spent?** We spend Christmas at home with kids and grandkids.

✳ **How many trees do you decorate?** One.

✳ **What's your favorite holiday tradition?** Attending Christmas Eve church service and listening to our talented music director sing "O Holy Night."

✳ **When do you start decorating? Undecorating?** I kick off the season by putting up outdoor lights right after Thanksgiving, before it gets too cold. My indoor decorating happens by the second week in December, and I undecorate the week after Christmas.

✳ **What was your favorite childhood toy?** A record player was my favorite, but I don't own it anymore.

Wool Snowman Door Hanging

BY LISA BONGEAN

No need to fill this holiday stocking with goodies; it's packed full in the making with a frosty snowman toting his own Christmas tree. A treasure of rich wools and embroidered details, this seasonal door hanging will greet your guests with a cheery how-do-you-do!

FINISHED SIZE: 7¾" × 24"

Materials

Wool requirements are based on wool that has been prewashed and lightly felted.

10" × 25" rectangle of black wool for stocking back and snowman's eyes

10" × 12" rectangle of brown herringbone wool for stocking

5" × 10" rectangle of light gray wool for tree

6" × 7" rectangle of ivory wool for snowman

5" × 5" square of medium green wool for scarf and holly leaves

3" × 9" rectangle of red stripe wool for snowman's heart and candy canes

3" × 7" rectangle of black-and-tan check wool for stocking cuff

3" × 3" square of dark red wool for hanging hearts and berries

2" × 2" square of gold wool for star

1" × 2" rectangle of orange wool for carrot nose

½ yard of 18"-wide lightweight paper-backed fusible web

Pearl cotton, size 12, in coordinating colors for appliqués

White marking pen (such as Clover brand)

Air-soluble marking pen

Chenille needle, size 24

Preparing the Appliqués

Appliqué patterns are on pages 67–69 and have been reversed for fusible appliqué.

1 Trace the appliqué patterns onto the fusible web, making sure to join the stocking pieces first, as indicated on the pattern. Lisa recommends cutting a piece of fusible web the same size as each wool piece. If you're cutting multiple shapes from one wool piece, trace all the shapes onto the corresponding fusible-web rectangle to ensure all of the pieces can be cut from the single piece of wool.

2 Fuse the traced shapes to the wrong side of each corresponding wool piece. Cut out the shapes on the drawn lines and remove the paper from the fusible web. Reserve the eye shapes to fuse and cut from the black wool scraps following step 4.

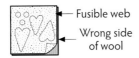

Fusible web

Wrong side of wool

Assembling the Door Hanging

1 Referring to the illustration below, position the tree, snowman, stocking, and cuff on the black rectangle. The slight tackiness of the fusible web will help keep the pieces in place. The shapes should overlap as needed rather than butt up against each other. Starting about 2" down from the top of the tree, fuse the shapes to the wrong side of the black rectangle, using generous steam as you press to avoid scorching the wool. The top 2" of the tree will be fused after the hanger is attached.

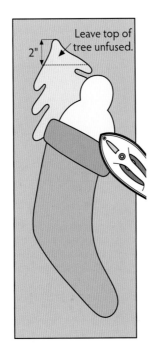

Leave top of tree unfused.

2"

2 Using the edge of the appliqué shapes as a guide, cut away the black wool around the perimeter of the tree, snowman, cuff, and stocking.

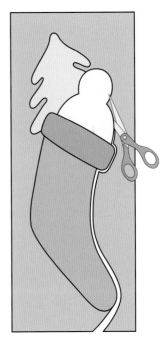

3 To create a hanger, thread a needle with a 4"-long strand of coordinating pearl cotton and tie a knot at the end. Insert the needle between the layers and bring it up through the black backing, about 2" from the treetop and ¾" from the left side. Insert the needle back down through the black backing, about ¾" from the right side, leaving a 2" loop. Knot the thread on the wrong side of the backing. Press the top of the tree to the backing to fuse, securing the ends of the loop between the layers. Tie a knot in the top of the loop.

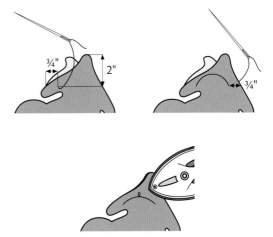

¾" 2"

¾"

4 Blanket stitch around the perimeter of the snowman, cuff, tree, and stocking using a chenille needle and coordinating pearl cotton. Lisa changed colors for each color of wool. For details on hand embroidery, see page 66.

5 Referring to the appliqué placement guide, position and fuse the remaining appliqué pieces onto the snowman, cuff, and stocking, making sure to layer the scarf before the carrot. Position the candy canes first, the holly leaves next, and the berries last.

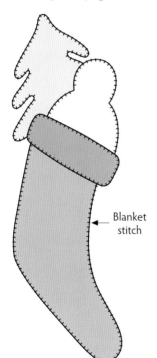

Blanket stitch

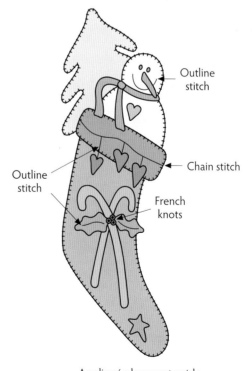

Outline stitch

Chain stitch

Outline stitch

French knots

Appliqué placement guide

Secrets from Santa

LISA BONGEAN

Oh the weather outside might be frightful in Wisconsin where Lisa Bongean (LisaBongean.com) lives, but inside it's always delightful as she stitches away on her snowman-filled stocking. We wonder, does the blanket stitch help keep her warm?

✳ **What is your favorite holiday treat?** Christmas cookies.

✳ **Do you send Christmas cards, holiday emails, texts, or tweets?** Christmas cards.

✳ **When do you open holiday gifts?** My husband, Nick, and I did "25 days of Christmas" last year. We opened one present each day in December till Christmas. It was lots of fun!

✳ **Home or on the road? Where are your holidays most often spent?** HOME.

✳ **How many trees do you decorate?** One.

✳ **What's your favorite holiday tradition?** Decorating cookies with my grandson!

✳ **When do you start decorating?** Right after the turkey is put away.

✳ **What was your favorite childhood toy?** A bike. And no, I don't still have it.

6 Blanket stitch around all the pieces in coordinating pearl cotton.

7 Use a white marking pen to draw a curvy line on the cuff and three vertical lines to the hanging hearts. Embroider over the markings using cream pearl cotton and a chain stitch for the curvy line and an outline stitch for the vertical lines. Draw a curved line on each holly leaf as a guide to embroider an outline stitch using coordinating pearl cotton. Using an air-soluble marker, draw a smile on the snowman and embroider an outline stitch using black pearl cotton. Stitch a small French knot in the center of each berry using coordinating pearl cotton.

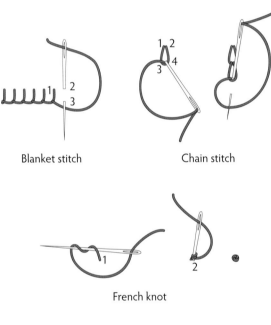

Blanket stitch   Chain stitch

French knot

Outline stitch

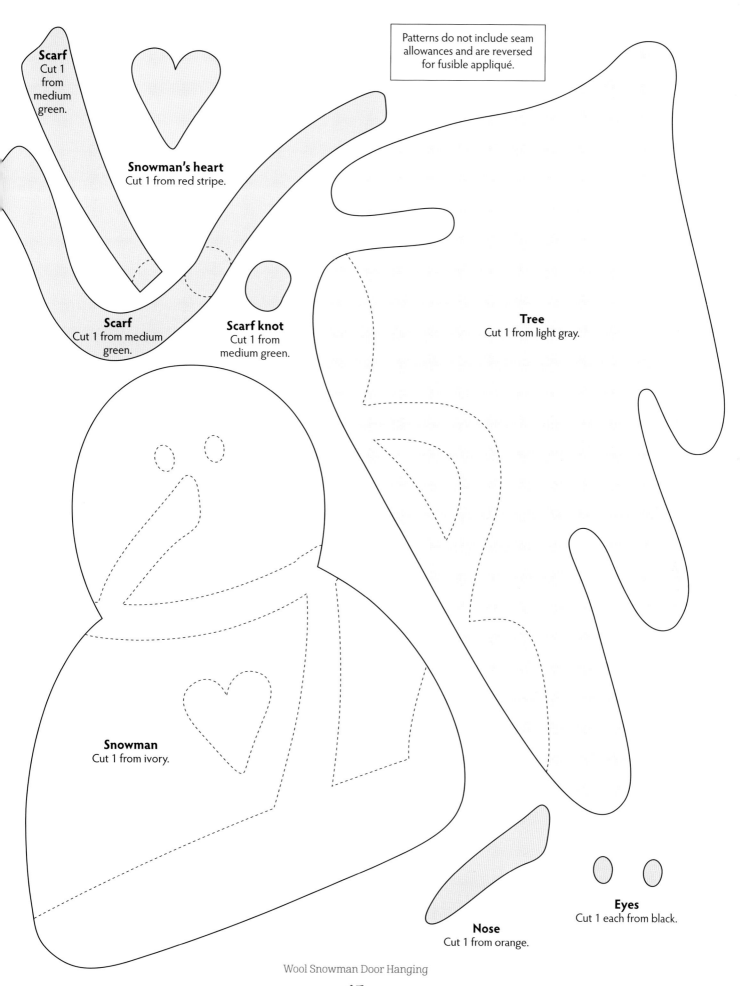

Scarf
Cut 1 from medium green.

Snowman's heart
Cut 1 from red stripe.

Scarf
Cut 1 from medium green.

Scarf knot
Cut 1 from medium green.

Tree
Cut 1 from light gray.

Snowman
Cut 1 from ivory.

Nose
Cut 1 from orange.

Eyes
Cut 1 each from black.

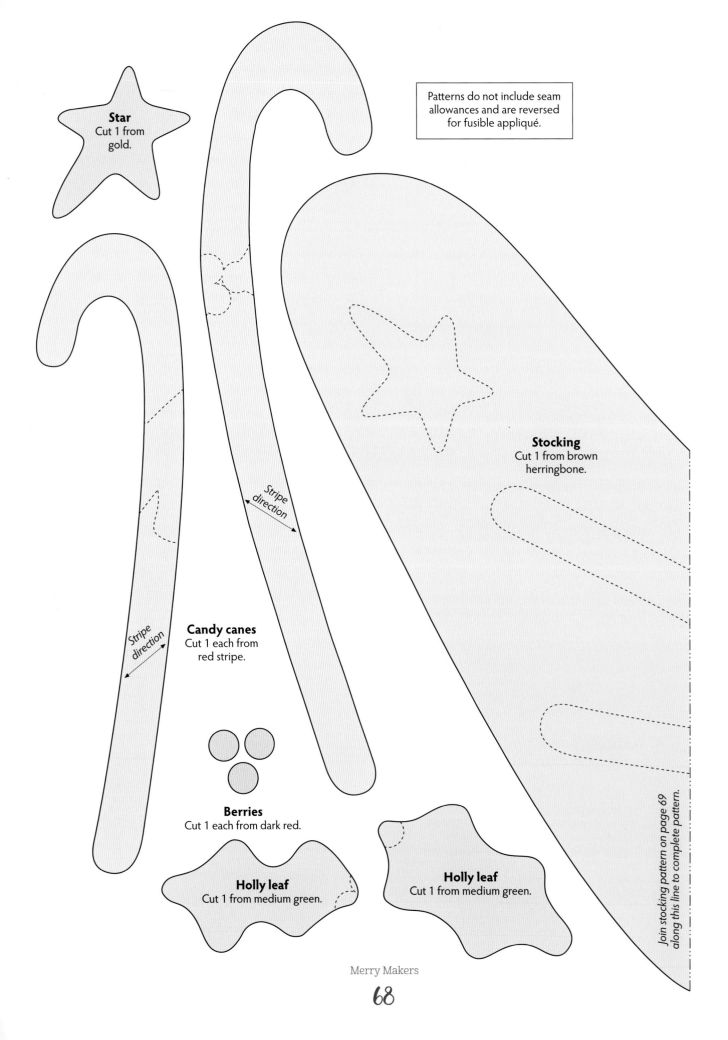

Star
Cut 1 from gold.

Patterns do not include seam allowances and are reversed for fusible appliqué.

Stocking
Cut 1 from brown herringbone.

Stripe direction

Stripe direction

Candy canes
Cut 1 each from red stripe.

Berries
Cut 1 each from dark red.

Holly leaf
Cut 1 from medium green.

Holly leaf
Cut 1 from medium green.

Join stocking pattern on page 69 along this line to complete pattern.

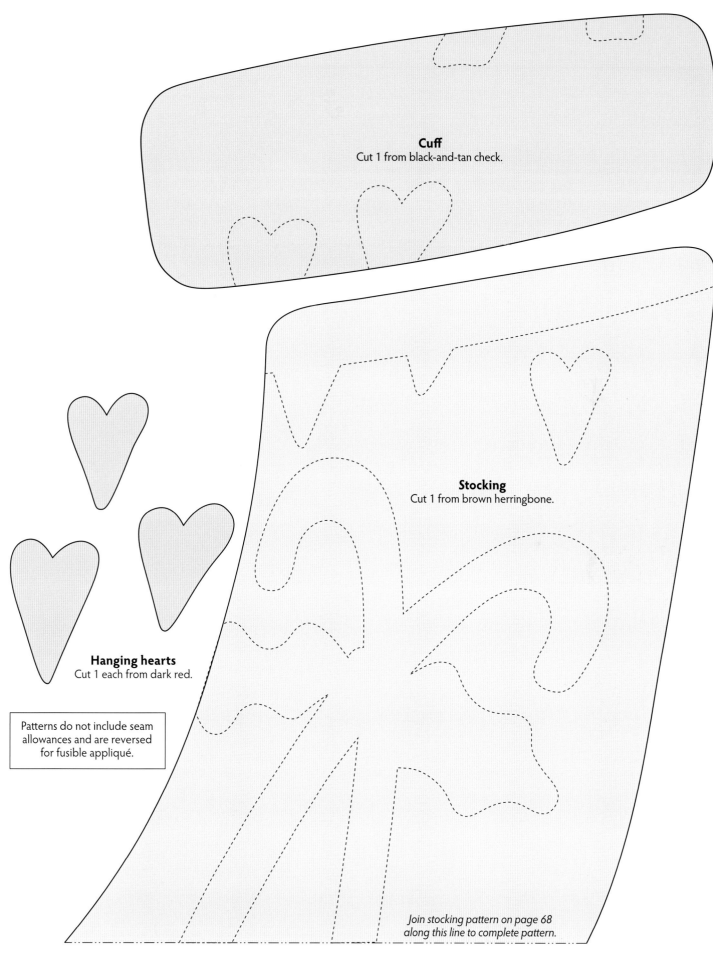

Cuff
Cut 1 from black-and-tan check.

Stocking
Cut 1 from brown herringbone.

Hanging hearts
Cut 1 each from dark red.

Patterns do not include seam allowances and are reversed for fusible appliqué.

Join stocking pattern on page 68 along this line to complete pattern.

Wool Snowman Door Hanging

Christmas Cabin Quilt

BY PAT SLOAN

Toss some logs on the fire, drop some marshmallows in your cocoa, and wrap this Christmas Cabin Quilt around your shoulders. Settling in for a blissful snowy evening has never been cozier.

FINISHED QUILT: 44½" × 60½"
FINISHED BLOCK: 12" × 12"

Materials

Yardage is based on 42"-wide fabric.

2 yards *total* of assorted cream batiks for blocks
1½ yards *total* of assorted red prints and batiks for blocks
1⅞ yards of red batik for appliqué background
⅓ yard of ivory batik for appliqués
⅓ yard of white solid for appliqués
½ yard of red print for binding
2⅞ yards of fabric for backing
51" × 67" piece of batting
1⅛ yards of 16"-wide lightweight paper-backed fusible web

Cutting

All measurements include ¼"-wide seam allowances.

From the cream batiks, cut a *total* of:
15 squares, 2½" × 2½" (A)
30 rectangles, 1½" × 4½" (C)
30 rectangles, 1½" × 6½" (E)
30 rectangles, 1½" × 8½" (G)
30 rectangles, 1½" × 10½" (I)
30 rectangles, 1½" × 12½" (K)

From the red prints and batiks, cut a *total* of:
30 rectangles, 1½" × 2½" (B)
30 rectangles, 1½" × 4½" (D)
30 rectangles, 1½" × 6½" (F)
30 rectangles, 1½" × 8½" (H)
30 rectangles, 1½" × 10½" (J)

Continued on page 72

Continued from page 71

From the *lengthwise* grain of the red batik for background, cut:

1 strip, 8½" × 60½"

From the red print for binding, cut:

6 strips, 2¼" × 42"

Making the Blocks

Press the seam allowances in the directions indicated by the arrows.

1 Sew red B rectangles to opposite sides of a cream A square. Make 15 units that measure 2½" × 4½", including seam allowances.

Make 15 units,
2½" × 4½".

2 Sew cream C rectangles to the top and bottom of each unit from step 1 to make 15 units. The units should measure 4½" square, including seam allowances.

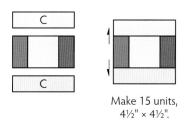

Make 15 units,
4½" × 4½".

3 Following the block assembly diagram, continue adding rectangles in alphabetical order, sewing the red rectangles to opposite sides of the unit and sewing the cream rectangles to the top and bottom. Make 15 blocks that measure 12½" square, including seam allowances.

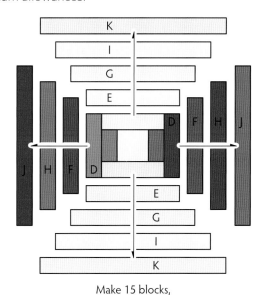

Make 15 blocks,
12½" × 12½".

Appliquéing the Snowflakes

For more detailed information about fusible appliqué, visit ShopMartingale.com/HowtoQuilt.

1 Using the patterns on page 75, trace 48 snowflake arms and 18 snowflake dots onto the paper-backing side of the fusible web. (This is twice the number as seen on the quilt top; Pat used a double layer to prevent the red background from showing through the white appliqués.) Cut out each shape, leaving about ¼" outside the traced line.

2 Fuse 24 snowflake arms and nine snowflake dots to the wrong side of the white solid. Fuse the remaining snowflake arms and dots to the wrong side of the ivory batik.

3 Cut out each shape exactly on the marked line.

4 Referring to the appliqué placement guide on page 74, position and fuse the white snowflake center dots and floating dots to the right side of the red 8½" × 60½" strip. Fuse the three white upper and three white lower snowflake arms to each white snowflake center. Fuse *only* the flat ends of the side snowflake arms to the center dot of each snowflake.

Donut Method

Pat cuts out the shapes from fusible web, leaving about ¼" outside of the traced line. Then she cuts out the center of the fusible web, leaving about ⅛" of fusible web inside the traced line. That way the shapes stay soft and pliable. For more details about Pat's method, see her book *Pat Sloan's Teach Me to Appliqué* (Martingale, 2015).

Secrets from Santa

PAT SLOAN

If Santa needs help packing his sleigh, he'd do well to hire Pat Sloan (PatSloan.com) as one of his elves, because we've not met many designers capable of packing more into a day, let alone a sleigh, than she does!

✷ **What is your favorite holiday treat?** Christmas cookies.

✷ **Do you send Christmas cards, holiday emails, texts, or tweets?** I still send a few cards, but I'm adding some of the other types of holiday greetings into my repertoire as well!

✷ **When do you open holiday gifts?** We open presents on Christmas Day.

✷ **Home or on the road? Where are your holidays most often spent?** We do both. We travel on Christmas Eve and then travel again on Christmas Day.

✷ **How many trees do you decorate?** Just one!

✷ **What's your favorite holiday tradition?** Our annual family photo on Christmas Eve with my husband's family.

✷ **When do you start decorating? Undecorating?** I decorate the day after Thanksgiving so I can enjoy my tree and decorations for the entire month. It all comes down around the end of the year.

✷ **What was your favorite childhood toy?** I'd have to say my Barbies. Any time I got a Barbie, it was my favorite thing to receive. I still have one Barbie that spoke German, because we lived in Germany when I got it.

5 Layer and fuse the upper and lower ivory batik snowflake arms directly on top of the corresponding white snowflake arms. Again, fuse *only* the flat ends of the side arms to the white snowflake center. Layer and fuse the ivory batik snowflake centers over the end of the fused arms. Layer and fuse the ivory batik floating dots on top of the corresponding white dots.

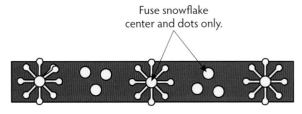

Fuse snowflake center and dots only.

Appliqué placement guide

6 Fold back the loose side arms onto the center of the snowflake and pin. These will be fused after the quilt top is assembled. Blanket stitch all of the fused snowflake pieces and floating dots to the red strip, unpinning and folding the loose arms out of the way as needed. Re-pin the arms before assembling the quilt top.

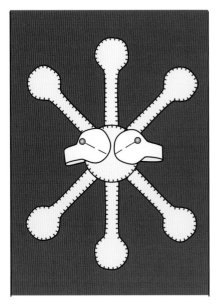

Assembling the Quilt Top

1 Join the blocks to make three columns of five blocks each as shown in the quilt assembly diagram below.

2 Sew a block column to each side of the snowflake panel.

3 Unpin the snowflake arms and fuse them to the quilt top. Blanket stitch to secure the edges of the appliqués.

4 Sew the remaining block column to the left side of the quilt top, making sure to align the intersections between the rectangles. The quilt top should measure 44½" × 60½".

Finishing

For more detailed information about any finishing steps, visit ShopMartingale.com/HowtoQuilt.

1 Layer the quilt top, batting, and backing, and quilt by hand or machine. Christmas Cabin Quilt is machine quilted with very light tan thread in a vertical pattern featuring a line with a bubble.

2 Use the red 2¼"-wide strips to make the binding, and then attach it to the quilt.

Quilt assembly

Snowflake dot
Make 9 from white solid
and 9 from ivory batik.

Snowflake arm
Make 24 from white solid
and 24 from ivory batik.

Peppermint-and-Pine Table Runner

BY SANDY KLOP

Before setting out the sweet treats this holiday season, make a table runner that's as yummy as the goodies you'll be serving on it. The pieces in the five hexagonal blocks, plus the setting triangles, are cut from templates so they fit together like a dream.

FINISHED RUNNER: 11¾" × 51½"
FINISHED BLOCK: 8¼" × 9½"

Materials

Yardage is based on 42"-wide fabric.

⅜ yard of red print for blocks

¾ yard of muslin for blocks, setting triangles, and border

⅓ yard of green diagonal stripe for binding*

⅞ yard of fabric for backing

18" × 58" piece of batting

Template plastic or cardstock

*To get the look of the featured binding using a regular stripe, cut strips on the bias. This will require ½ yard.

Cutting

All measurements include ¼"-wide seam allowances. Before you begin cutting, trace patterns A, B, and C on page 80 onto template plastic (or cardstock) and cut them out. Use the templates to trace and then cut the A, B, and C pieces from the fabrics indicated below.

From the red print, cut:
30 A pieces
5 squares, 2" × 2"

From the muslin, cut:
4 strips, 2" × 42"; crosscut *1 of the strips* into:
    2 rectangles, 2" × 8"
    2 rectangles, 2" × 6"
30 B pieces
8 C triangles

From the green stripe, cut:
4 strips, 2¼" × 42"

Making the Blocks

Press the seam allowances in the directions indicated by the arrows.

1 Sew six red A and six muslin B pieces together to make a block. Make five blocks that measure 8¾" from top to bottom and 10⅛" from point to point, including seam allowances.

 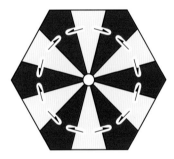

Make 5.

2 Trace the D circle on page 80 onto cardstock five times and cut out each circle. Trim off the corners of a red 2" square. Hand sew a running stitch just inside the outer edges of the red circle. Center a cardstock circle on the red circle. Pull the thread tails to gather the fabric over the cardstock template until it's evenly gathered. Tie off the threads to hold the gathering firmly in place. Make five circles.

Trim.

Make 5.

3 Press the circles well and let cool. Carefully remove the cardstock template. Tighten the gathering stitches to reshape the circle. Repeat for each circle.

4 Position a red circle in the center of each block and hand appliqué in place.

Make 5 blocks.

Assembling the Table Runner

1 Lay out the blocks and muslin C triangles as shown. Join the blocks and triangles in diagonal rows. Join the rows to make the table-runner center.

Table-runner assembly

2 Sew muslin 2" × 6" rectangles to the upper-left and lower-right edges of the table-runner top. Trim the ends at an angle. Sew muslin 2" × 8" rectangles to the upper-right and lower-left edges of the runner top. Trim.

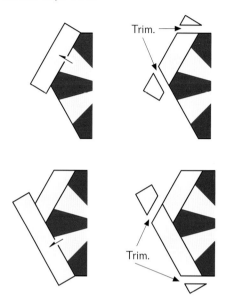

3 Join the muslin 2" × 42" strips end to end. Cut the pieced strip into two equal lengths and sew them to opposite sides of the table-runner top. Trim the ends of the side borders at an angle as shown.

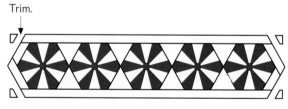

Adding borders

Finishing

For more detailed information about any finishing steps, visit ShopMartingale.com/HowtoQuilt.

1 Layer the runner top, batting, and backing, and quilt by hand or machine. Peppermint-and-Pine Table Runner is machine quilted with an allover meandering pattern in the muslin background.

2 Use the green 2¼"-wide strips to make the binding, and then attach it to the runner.

Secrets from Santa

SANDY KLOP

Sandy Klop (AmericanJane.com) has had visions of sugarplums dancing in her head, or at least peppermint swirls, with her cute-as-can-be holiday table runner.

✻ **What is your favorite holiday treat?** Caramel corn! A friend started me with a tin of her homemade caramel corn and it was so fabulous, I had to learn how to make it myself.

✻ **Do you send Christmas cards, holiday emails, texts, or tweets?** My husband writes and sends out our Christmas (or sometimes New Year's) greetings.

✻ **When do you open holiday gifts?** We open gifts first thing on Christmas morning and then have hot cinnamon rolls.

✻ **Home or on the road? Where are your holidays most often spent?** Always at home!

✻ **How many trees do you decorate?** Two—one small one in the front window for all to see and the other in the family room where we put all the presents.

✻ **What's your favorite holiday tradition?** When the kids were all home, we would invite other families to come and listen, and read a chapter of *The Best Christmas Pageant Ever* by Barbara Robinson.

✻ **What was your favorite childhood toy?** My hand-crank, clamp-to-the-table, Singer sewing machine! And I still have it!

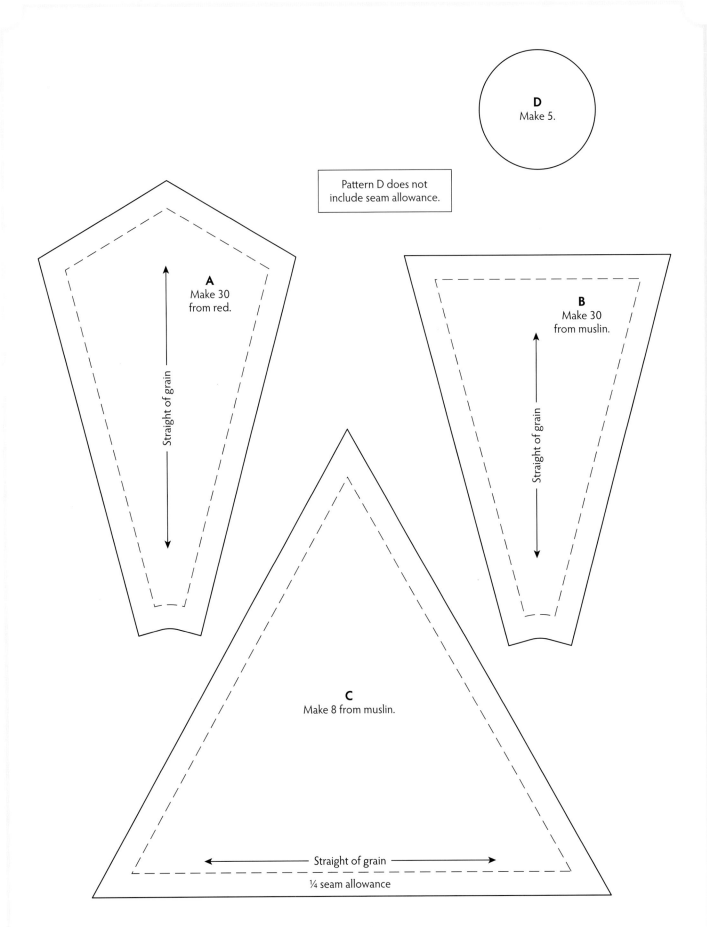

D
Make 5.

Pattern D does not include seam allowance.

A
Make 30 from red.

Straight of grain

B
Make 30 from muslin.

Straight of grain

C
Make 8 from muslin.

Straight of grain

¼ seam allowance

Vintage Star Runner

BY BONNIE OLAVESON

So many holiday prints. Choose your favorite for a border, pull out three different colors to make your Vintage Star blocks, and pick a coordinating print for your binding. Your Christmas table has never been merrier!

FINISHED RUNNER: 17" × 42½"

FINISHED BLOCK: 12" × 12"

Materials

Yardage is based on 42"-wide fabric. A fat eighth measures 9" × 21".

¾ yard of white print for blocks and inner border
3 fat eighths of assorted red prints for blocks
2 fat eighths of different aqua prints for blocks
1 fat eighth of green print for blocks
¼ yard of Christmas print for outer border
⅓ yard of red diagonal stripe for binding*
1⅜ yards of fabric for backing
23" × 49" piece of batting

*To get the look of the featured binding using a regular stripe, cut strips on the bias. This will require ½ yard.

Cutting

All measurements include ¼"-wide seam allowances.

From the white print, cut:
3 strips, 3½" × 42"; crosscut into:
    12 squares, 3½" × 3½"
    24 rectangles, 2" × 3½"
1 strip, 2⅜" × 42"; crosscut into 12 squares,
    2⅜" × 2⅜". Cut the squares in half diagonally
    to yield 24 triangles.
2 strips, 2" × 42"; crosscut into 36 squares, 2" × 2"
4 strips, 1¼" × 42"; crosscut *2 of the strips* into
    4 strips, 1¼" × 12½"

From *each* of 1 red, 1 aqua, and the green print, cut:
1 square, 3½" × 3½" (3 total)
8 squares, 2" × 2" (24 total)

Continued on page 83

Continued on page 83

Continued from page 81

From *each* of 1 aqua and 2 red prints, cut:

4 rectangles, 2" × 3½" (12 total)

4 squares, 2⅜" × 2⅜"; cut the squares in half
  diagonally to yield 8 triangles (24 total)

8 squares, 2" × 2" (24 total)

From the Christmas print, cut:

3 strips, 2" × 42"

From the red stripe, cut:

4 strips, 2¼" × 42"

Making the Blocks

Instructions are for making one block. Press the
seam allowances in the directions indicated by
the arrows.

1 Sew a white triangle to a red triangle, right sides
together, to make a half-square-triangle unit.
Make eight matching half-square-triangle units that
measure 2" square, including seam allowances.

Make 8 units,
2" × 2".

2 Using the same red used in step 1, draw a
diagonal line from corner to corner on the

wrong side of eight red 2" squares. Place a marked
square on one end of a white 2" × 3½" rectangle,
right sides together, and stitch on the drawn line.
Trim the seam allowance to ¼"; press. Place a
second marked square on the opposite end of the
rectangle; stitch, trim, and press to make a flying-
geese unit as shown. Make four matching units that
measure 2" × 3½", including seam allowances.

Make 4 units,
2" × 3½".

3 Repeat step 2 using eight matching aqua 2"
squares and four white 2" × 3½" rectangles to
make four flying-geese units.

Make 4 units,
2" × 3½".

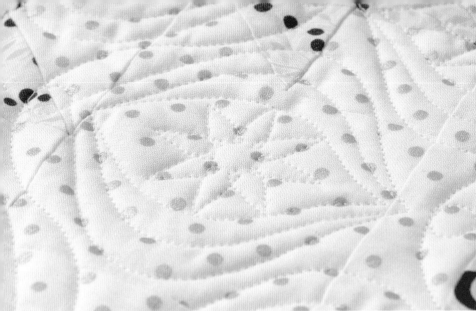

4 Arrange two red half-square-triangle units, one red flying-geese unit from step 2, one red 2" × 3½" rectangle, and two white 2" squares in two rows as shown. The red print should be the same throughout. Sew the pieces together into rows. Join the rows to make a star-point unit. Make four matching units that measure 3½" × 6½", including seam allowances.

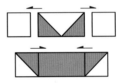
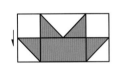

Make 4 units,
3½" × 6½".

5 Arrange four aqua flying-geese units from step 3, four white 2" squares, and one aqua 3½" square in three rows as shown. The aqua print should be the same in both the flying-geese units and the square. Sew the pieces together into rows. Join the rows to make a center-star unit that measures 6½" square, including seam allowances.

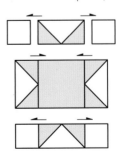
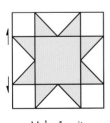

Make 1 unit,
6½" × 6½".

6 Lay out four white 3½" squares, four matching star-point units, and the center-star unit in three rows as shown. Sew the pieces together into rows. Join the rows to make a block that measures 12½" square, including seam allowances.

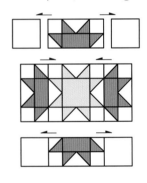
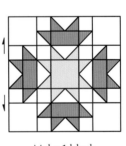

Make 1 block,
12½" × 12½".

7 Repeat steps 1–6 to make one block with red star points and a green center star, and one with aqua star points and a red center star.

Assembling the Table Runner

1 Lay out the blocks and two white 1¼" × 12½" strips as shown in the table-runner assembly diagram on page 85. Join the blocks and strips to make a row that measures 12½" × 38", including seam allowances.

2 Sew white 1¼" × 12½" strips to the short edges of the row. Measure the length of the table-runner top, including the borders just added. Trim the two white 1¼" × 42" strips to that measurement. Sew the strips to the long edges of the table runner to complete the inner border. The table runner should measure 14" × 39½", including seam allowances.

3 Measure the width of the table-runner top. Cut two strips to that measurement from the Christmas print strips. Join the strips to the short edges of the runner. Measure the length of the table runner, including the borders just added. Cut two strips to that measurement from the remaining Christmas print strips, piecing the strips if needed. Sew the strips to the long edges of the table runner to complete the outer border. The table runner should measure 17" × 42½".

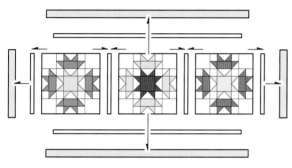

Table-runner assembly

Finishing

For more detailed information about any finishing steps, visit ShopMartingale.com/HowtoQuilt.

1 Layer the runner top, batting, and backing, and quilt by hand or machine. Vintage Star Runner is machine quilted with star shapes surrounded by echoing curves.

2 Use the red 2¼"-wide strips to make the binding, and then attach it to the runner.

Secrets from Santa

BONNIE OLAVESON

We're not sure exactly where Bonnie Olaveson (CottonWay.bigcartel.com) spends her wintertime, but it must be close to Santa's workshop because she's in Idaho-ho-ho.

✳ **What is your favorite holiday treat?** Anything with chocolate and nuts. Toffee, fudge, peanut clusters, it's all good! I definitely have a sweet tooth.

✳ **Do you send Christmas cards, holiday emails, texts, or tweet?** It depends on what's happening and how much time I have. I mix it up every year.

✳ **When do you open holiday gifts?** Now that all of my children are married, we open gifts on Christmas Day or whenever we can get together.

✳ **Home or on the road? Where are your holidays most often spent?** We usually spend Christmas Eve and Christmas Day at home and then go to our family cabin the day after Christmas and stay until New Year's Day.

✳ **How many trees do you decorate?** I decorate one tree at home that's a little more fancy and decorate one at our cabin that's more rustic.

✳ **What's your favorite holiday tradition?** The grandkids get new pajamas every year and open them on Christmas Eve. On Christmas morning everyone waits on the stairs so we can take the annual photo and then all go into our family room together to see what Santa brought.

✳ **When do you start decorating? Undecorating?** I decorate after Thanksgiving and take everything down after New Year's.

✳ **What was your favorite childhood toy?** One Christmas my sister and I got matching dolls. Mine had brown hair and hers had blonde. My mom made clothes and flannel quilts for them.

Holiday Pinnies

BY CARRIE NELSON

Thirty minutes. An hour if you quilt it. Two hours if you overthink it. That's the great thing about making pincushions—the almost-instant gratification of making something start-to-finish using leftover bits of your favorite fabrics.

Materials

Yardage is based on 42"-wide fabric. Materials are for all five pinnies.

⅔ yard *total* of assorted white, red, green, gray, and aqua print scraps for pinnie fronts and backing

8" × 30" piece of needle-punched batting

Neutral-colored thread: 50 weight for machine piecing, 40 weight for closing stuffed pincushion by hand, and 80 weight (by Aurifil) for machine quilting

Crushed walnut shells, play sand, or other stuffing

Crushed Walnut Shells

Crushed walnut shells (also called hulls) are great for filling pin cushions. They're available at pet stores, as they're sold as cage litter for lizards and other critters. Finding your preferred firmness level may take an experiment or two, but you can unstitch the opening to add or remove fill.

To pack your pinnies full, insert a chopstick or pencil and wiggle it around to help the shells settle. Add more fill. Repeat until your pinnie is the desired firmness.

General Pinnie Tips

✻ All seam allowances are a scant ¼" unless otherwise specified.

✻ With the exception of the triangles on the flying geese, all the seam allowances are pressed open. Pressing open makes the top of the pincushion flatter and the machine quilting easier.

✻ For pincushions with borders, consider cutting the borders a little wider than needed so that the quilted piece can be trimmed straight.

✻ Quilting is optional, but pincushions look fabulous when they're quilted.

✻ Pinnies work best with thin, flat battings— cotton, blends, bamboo, and so on. Use the weight recommended for hand quilting. Cut the batting about 1" larger than the pieced pincushion top. The batting layer eliminates the need for lining and gives the finished pinnie a smooth look and feel. Lay the pieced top on the batting and press it flat.

✻ Use straight-line quilting, either in straight parallel lines or in a grid. You might also like edgestitch quilting for the pincushions; stitch approximately ⅛" from the seamline.

✻ Use whatever leftover pieces of backing fabric you have on hand; leftover pieces from quilt backings are perfect. You can quilt the backing piece with a batting layer, but that, too, is optional. If you're not going to quilt the backing, adhere a piece of fusible interfacing to the wrong side of the backing fabric for stability and appearance.

✻ Find finishing instructions for all the pinnies on page 94.

✻ The most important instruction: these are supposed to be fun. Perfection is highly overrated, and pinnies are a terrific way to practice piecing "small."

House Pinnie

FINISHED PINNIE: 3½" × 4½"

Cutting

All measurements include ¼"-wide seam allowances.

From the white print scraps, cut:
2 squares, 1¾" × 1¾"
4 rectangles, 1" × 4"

From the red print scraps, cut:
1 rectangle, 1¾" × 3"
1 rectangle, 1½" × 2"

From the green print scraps, cut:
2 rectangles, 1¼" × 2¾"
1 rectangle, 1¼" × 1½"

From the backing fabric, cut:
1 rectangle, 4" × 5"

Making the House Pinnie

Press the seam allowances in the directions indicated by the arrows.

1 Draw a diagonal line from corner to corner on the wrong side of the white 1¾" squares. Place a marked square on one end of the red 1¾" × 3" rectangle, right sides together, and stitch on the drawn line. Trim the seam allowance to ¼"; press. Place the second marked square on the opposite end of the rectangle, right sides together. Stitch, trim, and press to make the flying-geese roof unit, which should measure 1¾" × 3".

Make 1 unit,
1¾" × 3".

2 Join the green 1¼" × 1½" rectangle to the top of the red 1½" × 2" rectangle. Join the green 1¼" × 2¾" rectangles to each side of the pieced rectangle to make the house unit. Sew the roof unit to the house unit to make a unit that measures 3" × 4", including seam allowances.

Make 1 unit,
3" × 4".

3 Sew white 1" × 4" rectangles to the sides of the house unit. Sew the remaining white 1" × 4" rectangles to the top and bottom of the house unit to complete the pinnie front, which should measure 4" × 5", including seam allowances.

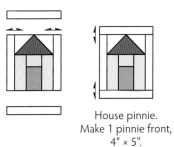

House pinnie.
Make 1 pinnie front,
4" × 5".

4 Layer the pinnie front with batting. Machine quilt and trim the finished pinnie front to 4" × 5". Refer to "Pincushion Finishing" on page 94 to complete the pinnie.

Making Flying Geese Pinnie A

Press the seam allowances in the directions indicated by the arrows.

1 Using the white squares and red rectangles, make flying-geese units, referring to step 1 on page 89. Make five units that measure 1½" × 2½".

Make 5 units,
1½" × 2½".

2 Join the flying-geese units to make a row that measures 2½" × 5½".

Make 1 unit,
2½" × 5½".

3 Sew green 1" × 5½" rectangles to the sides of the row to complete the pinnie front.

Flying Geese Pinnie A.
Make 1 pinnie front,
3½" × 5½".

4 Layer the pinnie front with batting. Machine quilt and trim the finished pinnie front to 3½" × 5½". Refer to "Pincushion Finishing" on page 94 to complete the pinnie.

Flying Geese Pinnie A

FINISHED PINNIE: 3" × 5"

Cutting

All measurements include ¼"-wide seam allowances. Instructions are for one pinnie. Reverse the cutting dimensions for the red and green scraps for a second pinnie.

From the white print scraps, cut:
10 squares, 1½" × 1½"

From the red print scraps, cut:
5 rectangles, 1½" × 2½"

From the green print scraps, cut:
2 rectangles, 1" × 5½"

From the backing fabric, cut:
1 rectangle, 3½" × 5½"

Flying Geese Pinnie B

FINISHED PINNIE: 2½" × 6"

Cutting

All measurements include ¼"-wide seam allowances.

From the gray print scraps, cut:
16 squares, 1¼" × 1¼"

From the red print scraps, cut:
4 rectangles, 1¼" × 2"

From the green print scraps, cut:
4 rectangles, 1¼" × 2"

From the white print scraps, cut:
2 rectangles, 1" × 6½"

From the backing fabric, cut:
1 rectangle, 3" × 6½"

Making Flying Geese Pinnie B

Press the seam allowances in the directions indicated by the arrows.

1 Using the gray squares and red rectangles, make flying-geese units, referring to step 1 on page 89. Make four units that measure 1¼" × 2".

2 Use the remaining gray squares and the green rectangles to make four flying-geese units that measure 1¼" × 2".

3 Join the flying-geese units to make a row that measures 2" × 6½", including seam allowances.

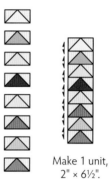

Make 1 unit,
2" × 6½".

4 Sew the white rectangles to the sides to complete the pinnie front, which should measure 3" × 6½", including seam allowances.

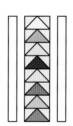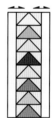

Flying Geese Pinnie B.
Make 1 pinnie front,
3" × 6½".

5 Layer the pinnie front with batting. Machine quilt and trim the finished pinnie front to 3" × 6½". Refer to "Pincushion Finishing" on page 94 to complete the pinnie.

Improv-ish Pinnie

FINISHED PINNIE: 3" × 6"

Cutting

All measurements include ¼"-wide seam allowances.

From the red, white, and green print scraps, cut:
15 rectangles, 1" × 5" (Leftover charm-square rectangles work perfectly.)

From the backing fabric, cut:
1 rectangle, 3½" × 6½"

Making the Improv-ish Pinnie

Press the seam allowances in the directions indicated by the arrows.

1 Lay out the red, white, and green rectangles in the desired order. Join 14 of the rectangles in pairs along their long edges to make seven 1½" × 5" units. One rectangle will be left over.

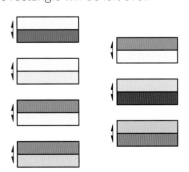

2 Use a ruler and rotary cutter to cut each unit off-kilter as shown. Each unit should be approximately 1¼" × 4½"; vary the angle and direction of the cut from one unit to another. The width of the rectangle can vary but try to keep the length at least 4½". The cut can go across the seam.

3 Join the off-kilter strips. Add the remaining single rectangle to complete the pinnie front.

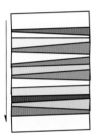

4 Layer the pinnie front with batting. Quilt as desired and trim the finished pinnie front to 3½" × 6½". The length and width can vary, but make sure to cut your backing and batting pieces accordingly. Refer to "Pincushion Finishing" on page 94 to complete the pinnie.

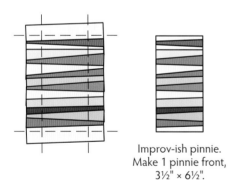

Improv-ish pinnie.
Make 1 pinnie front,
3½" × 6½".

consisting of one red rectangle and two red squares. Make two green groups, each consisting of one green rectangle and two green squares. These groups will form the complete crosses on the pinnie front.

2 Referring to the photo at left, lay out the groups from step 1, four remaining rectangles, and 14 of the remaining squares in eight rows, making sure to keep the groups from step 1 in the arrangement as shown. Some of the 2" rectangles will need to be shortened to measure 1½", but until the pieces are arranged by color, you don't know which ones will need to be trimmed.

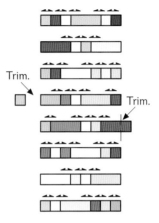

Plus Squares Pinnie

FINISHED PINNIE: 4" × 4"

Cutting

All measurements include ¼"-wide seam allowances.

From *each* of 4 white, 4 red, and 5 green print scraps, cut:
1 rectangle, 1" × 2" (13 total)
3 squares, 1" × 1" (39 total; 9 will be extra)

From the backing fabric, cut:
1 square, 4½" × 4½"

Making the Plus Squares Pinnie

Press the seam allowances in the directions indicated by the arrows.

1 As you make the following groups, all the prints within each group should match. Make four white groups, each consisting of one white rectangle with two white squares. Make two red groups, each

3 Join the squares and rectangles into rows. Join the rows to complete the pinnie front. Trim and square up the pinnie front to measure 4½" square.

Plus Squares pinnie.
Make 1 pinnie front,
4½" × 4½".

4 Layer the pinnie front with batting. Machine quilt and trim the finished pinnie front to 4½" square. Refer to "Pincushion Finishing" on page 94 to complete the pinnie.

Secrets from Santa

CARRIE NELSON

As for Naughty and Nice lists, Carrie Nelson's dad once told her she was on the "The Jury is Still Out List." Well, Carrie, with these cute pincushions we're pinning your name on the "Nice" list. Now, can we each have one?

✳ **What is your favorite holiday treat?** All of it—and I don't mean just the food! I love all of the seasonal, limited-edition "stuff." From scented candles to candies, the fancy cheeses that show up in every store, and of course, the seasonal breads and cookies.

✳ **Do you send Christmas cards, holiday emails, texts, or tweets?** I've been a texter the past few years, but I'd like to get back to sending a few Christmas cards. I love getting them, so it seems only fair to send them.

✳ **When do you open holiday gifts?** If a wonderful-looking package arrives at my apartment and it's just me . . . right away. My family tradition was Christmas Eve, but now I save gifts to open Christmas Day.

✳ **Home or on the road? Where are your holidays most often spent?** In recent years, it's been at my brother's home with a big group of his friends in for dinner.

✳ **What's your favorite holiday tradition?** I enjoy the hustle and bustle of grocery shopping a day or two before Christmas. I also love the lights of a Christmas tree when the room is dark and it's quiet . . . except for maybe some soft Christmas music. And I can't forget Christmas music. All. Day. Long. For weeks.

Pincushion Finishing

Refer to the specific pinnie instructions to complete the pinnie fronts.

1 Layer the backing with the batting, or stabilize with a fusible interfacing.

2 Machine baste ⅛" from the bottom edge on the pinnie front and back to help reinforce the edge when you close the stuffed pinnie.

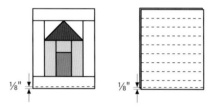

3 Layer the quilted pinnie front and back, right sides together. Using a scant ¼" seam allowance, stitch around the perimeter of the pinnie, leaving a 1½" opening along the bottom edge. Backstitch across the corners and trim the seam allowances to approximately ⅛".

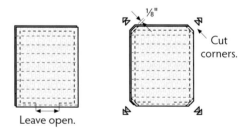

4 Carefully turn the pinnie right side out. Use a large knitting needle or crochet hook to carefully push out the corners and sides. Stuff the pinnie to the desired firmness.

5 Stitch in one direction to close the opening, and then stitch back in the other direction to secure.

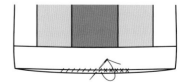

Meet the Moda All-Stars

LISA BONGEAN

A designer for Moda Fabrics, Lisa loves quilting, gardening, reading, and hunting for antiques. She and her husband, Nick, own Primitive Gatherings Quilt Shop and travel to quilting shows where Lisa teaches and shares her designs. You can find her at LisaBongean.com.

BETSY CHUTCHIAN

Betsy is an author, a designer for Moda Fabrics, and the cofounder of the 19th-Century Patchwork Divas. She developed a passionate interest in fabric, quilts, sewing, and history as a child. She enjoys sharing her passion for reproducing 19th-century quilts. Visit BetsysBestQuiltsandMore.blogspot.com.

JANE DAVIDSON

Jane's love affair with quilting started when she was a teenager. She loves to add vibrant prints and textures to her quilts. Together, Jane and Pat Sloan created The Splendid Sampler Sew-Along. Jane enjoys traveling to teach and meeting enthusiastic quilters from all over the world. Visit QuiltJane.com.

KARLA EISENACH

Karla and her daughters, Lisa Burnett and Susan Kendrick, are the creative minds behind Sweetwater, a design company in Colorado. Sweetwater started out as a scrapbook business and has now evolved to include fabric design, quilt patterns, kits, and more. Discover the latest at TheSweetwaterCo.com.

JOANNA FIGUEROA

For Joanna, quilting is the perfect combination of art and practicality. Joanna and her team at Fig Tree and Company produce quilting and sewing patterns, block-of-the-month programs, and kits, and have also designed countless fabric lines for Moda Fabrics. Find out more at FigTreeQuilts.com.

BARBARA GROVES AND MARY JACOBSON

Sisters Barbara and Mary make up the popular design team of Me and My Sister Designs. In addition to a line of quilt patterns, they have designed several fabric lines for Moda Fabrics. Visit MeandMySisterDesigns.com.

SANDY KLOP

Sandy was trained as an art teacher and began quilting in 1979 while living in Iran and then Saudi Arabia, teaching at an American school. In 2002 she began creating her own patterns under the name American Jane Patterns and was soon designing for Moda Fabrics. Visit AmericanJane.com.

SHERRI McCONNELL

Sherri received her first sewing machine when she was about 10 years old and has been sewing clothing and home-decor items ever since. After receiving a "gentle push" from her grandmother, she branched out into quilting and hasn't stopped. You can find Sherri at AQuiltingLife.com.

JO MORTON

Jo is a celebrated author, Moda fabric designer, and teacher who is known for making present-day quilts look like quilts from the past. Well known for her "Jo's Little Women Club" patterns, she is the author of *Jo's Little Favorites* (Martingale, 2016). Visit JoMortonQuilts.com.

CARRIE NELSON

Carrie's fans know her by her pattern-designer name, Miss Rosie. At Moda, Carrie is the guru of social media (perhaps not her official title, but that's what she's all about), but she still slips into her Miss Rosie mode from time to time. No matter what you call her, you'll call her patchwork patterns brilliant!

BONNIE OLAVESON

A pattern and fabric designer, Bonnie started her company, Cotton Way, in 1990. She has now created more than 300 patterns and is part of the mother-daughter team that designs the Bonnie and Camille fabric line for Moda Fabrics. She and her daughter enjoy blending trendy with traditional. Visit Bonnie at CottonWay.com.

BRENDA RIDDLE

Brenda creates quilts, embroidery, punchneedle designs, and more for crafters of all levels. At Brenda Riddle Designs, home of Acorn Quilt and Gift Company, the goal is to provide designs for handmade "works of heart" that will become treasures. Visit AcornQuiltandGiftCompany.com.

KATHY SCHMITZ

Kathy made her first quilt at age 13 on her grandmother's treadle sewing machine. She grew up drawing, painting, and sewing, and went on to become a graphic designer. In 2002 she founded Kathy Schmitz Studio, and her illustrations were a huge success. See the latest at KathySchmitz.com.

PAT SLOAN

Pat is a quilt designer, author, teacher, radio/podcast show producer and host, and fabric designer. Her passion for quilting is limitless. Pat travels around the world teaching and hosts several Internet groups of quilters where they share on a daily basis what they make. You can find her at PatSloan.com.

COREY YODER

A quilty mom of two girls and wife to one great husband, Corey enjoys playing with fabric in the form of quilts and quilt design. You can find her at CorianderQuilts.com.